Teamwork Test Prep

MATH

GRADE

8

by Drew Johnson and
Cynthia Johnson

Illustrations by Marty Bucella

Carson-Dellosa Publishing Company, Inc.
Greensboro, North Carolina

Credits

Authors: Drew Johnson and Cynthia Johnson
Editors: Kelly Morris Huxmann, Karen Seberg, and Amy Gamble
Layout Design: Mark Conrad
Production: River Road Graphics
Inside Illustrations: Marty Bucella
Cover Design: Annette Hollister-Papp

ISBN: 0-88724-274-X

 **Table of Contents**

Introduction 4

Chapter 1: Understanding Your State's Tests 5
The No Child Left Behind Act 5
How State Assessment Tests Are Developed 6
Checklist: What You Need to Know about Your State's Tests 7
The Information You Need: Resources for State Standards and Assessment 8

Chapter 2: Introducing the Tests to Your Students 13
The Coach Approach 13
Devising a Game Plan 15
Cross Training in the Classroom 16
The Mental Game: Motivation, Metacognition, and Modeling 17
How Coaching Looks in the Classroom 17

Chapter 3: Identifying Problem Areas 18
Checklist: Evaluating Your Students' Testing Savvy 18
Diagnostic Math Test—Grade 8 19

Chapter 4: Test-Taking Skills and Strategies 27
Reducing Test Anxiety 27
Pacing 29
Strategic Guessing 32
Math Strategies 34
Top Five Test-Taking Tips for Students 35
Reproducibles for Test-Taking Skills and Strategies 36

Chapter 5: Skill-Building Math Activities 43
Matrix of Skills Addressed in Math Activities 44
Math Activities 46
Reproducibles for Math Activities 72

Chapter 6: Practice Math Test—Grade 8 91

Answer Key 112

 # Introduction

Across the country, thousands of students and teachers spend countless hours preparing for state standardized tests. This focus on repetitive, high-intensity preparation can increase student anxiety, cause "burnout," and lead students to develop strong negative feelings about testing—all undesirable effects that can ultimately hurt students' test performance.

Teamwork Test Prep offers a change of pace. This book provides fun, creative group activities that sharpen students' test-taking abilities, build their confidence, instill positive attitudes toward the tests they are facing, and provide them with a supportive network of classmates who share their goals.

Teamwork Test Prep is an effective alternative to the drills and drudgery often associated with the process of getting students ready for standardized tests. It provides everything you need to transform test preparation from a necessary chore into a group experience that is rewarding in its own right. Here is what you will find inside this book:

✗ A short history of the rise of state testing programs

✗ A list of resources where you can find more information about your state's tests and learning standards

✗ An explanation of our unique "teamwork" approach to test preparation and your key role as "coach"

✗ A short, diagnostic math test to measure your students' current abilities and gauge their progress

✗ Important test-taking skills and strategies that students can really use

✗ Engaging group activities specifically designed to hone important math skills

✗ A practice test to help students prepare for the real thing

Use *Teamwork Test Prep* as a self-contained test preparation program, or supplement your existing program with the activities and diagnostics in this book. Either approach is sure to give your students a boost—in their scores, spirits, and confidence!

Understanding Your State's Tests

Understanding the issues involved with state assessment tests is the first step in preparing your students for success. Although standards may vary from state to state, there are many important issues that are common to all states when it comes to standardized testing. The practical information found in this chapter can be used by teachers anywhere in the United States. It includes:

- ✗ The basic components of the No Child Left Behind Act
- ✗ An overview of the test development process at the state level
- ✗ A checklist of questions to help you familiarize yourself with your state's tests
- ✗ Valuable resources you can use to gather more information about your state's tests

The No Child Left Behind Act

Passed in January 2002, the No Child Left Behind Act (NCLB) represents the federal government's most recent plan for education reform. The centerpiece of the law mandates annual testing in math and reading, beginning in 2005, for all public school students in grades three through eight. Although this is a federal mandate, the government has not established a concurrent set of national standards that all states must follow. Instead, states have the flexibility to create their own "statewide accountability systems." Within these systems, each state typically:

- ✗ Sets academic standards in each content area for what students should learn and master at each grade level
- ✗ Develops tests that are aligned with the state standards
- ✗ Uses those tests to collect objective data to analyze how students are doing (Often this data is delineated to show how various socioeconomic subsets are faring in the educational system)
- ✗ Makes improvements in curriculum, instruction, and assessment based on test results

Whatever systems the state chooses to develop and follow, it is ultimately held responsible for the performance of its students. Students must perform at a proficient level—according to each state's standards—within 12 years of NCLB's enactment. Each state must also share its data or test results with local communities in the form of reports. These reports are designed to inform parents and other stakeholders of how student learning is measuring up to the state's standards and educational goals. Consequences of the testing results may differ from state to state. In one state, a low-performing district that shows no improvement might have its superintendent replaced, while in another, a school with continued "failing" grades might find itself taken over by the state education agency.

Since many states already have some form of state testing in place, the passage of No Child Left Behind has not drastically changed current testing patterns. Tests are being revamped, however, to meet NCLB requirements. Since each state has flexibility in setting its own standards, the tests students will take are likely to reflect what they may already know or are currently learning. For example, a standardized math test established for eighth graders in Wisconsin would be relevant for students in that state, but not necessarily for eighth graders in Arizona.

How State Assessment Tests Are Developed

The first step in developing state assessment tests is to establish learning standards. This helps ensure equal learning opportunities for all students and, thus, equal opportunities for academic achievement. Standards are usually divided by grade level and content area, or discipline; and some are further divided by course number or subdiscipline. These standards form the basis of the scope and sequence of skills assessed, and, in some cases, they delineate actual content covered, as in social studies or science.

Standards developed in each state set the tone for instruction and achievement. Most state standards reflect carefully derived expectations of what students should know and be able to do at a specific grade level. These expectations of proficiency also establish curriculum frameworks. Educators use these standards as a scaffolding to determine the skills, content, and processes that students should learn.

After the standards are established, the actual test development process begins. Although the process varies from state to state, test development generally goes through several stages. Each state department of education or state educational agency has a specific internal department or division dedicated to curriculum development and assessment. This group of professional educators first evaluates any previous state assessments to see how well they measure current or newly adopted standards. Then, through analysis of similar or previously administered exams and current assessment research, these educators develop testing blueprints to best represent the core standards and essential elements of the curriculum.

The next stage for most states involves developing a field test based on the blueprints. Field tests are written and administered to try out items that may be used later on actual tests. After the field tests have been administered, review committees evaluate the results to determine the appropriateness, accuracy, and alignment of test items.

Benchmark tests may also be developed to set the scoring goals for new assessments or standards. Like field tests, these tests are scored and recorded, but are not used for accountability purposes at the district, school, or student level. These benchmark tests are used to see how well students will perform on the final tests and to help guide instruction.

The actual writing of the tests can vary depending on the state. Some states develop the tests completely within their own education departments. Assessment specialists review and revise test items, which are written by professional item writers hired independently by the education department. Some states, such as Texas and New York, hire former or current teachers to develop test items based on blueprints created by their education departments.

In other states, the tests are outsourced and written by professional educational testing companies that have contracted with the state. Test items are written by company-hired professional writers or, in some cases, by professional writers collaborating with education department staff. These writers use the previously developed test blueprints as guidelines for writing. Each item is written to measure specific content standards and then reviewed by the state's education department for alignment and accuracy.

Once benchmark tests have been developed and administered to students, a passing standard is established on the basis of the results. This passing standard is used to compare how well students should perform versus how well they actually do perform on the real tests.

Finally, the real tests are developed and administered to students. If students do not perform at or above the passing standard, schools use the results to examine factors that may help improve students' scores and, along with them, academic achievement.

Checklist: What You Need to Know about Your State's Tests

Having the information you need about your own state's tests is crucial to your students' achievement. Luckily, this information is readily available. Use the following checklist of questions as a guide in learning about your state's standards and assessment tests:

- [ ] What are the learning standards for each major content area per grade level?
- [ ] What is the most current form of state assessment test administered at each grade level?
- [ ] What is the state's time frame for developing and administering new assessment tests?
- [ ] What is the schedule of testing dates for each grade level?
- [ ] How are the standards assessed for each test at each grade level?
- [ ] What scoring and rating systems are used for the tests?
- [ ] How and when are testing "report cards" disseminated?
- [ ] Is there any additional pre- and post-testing data available?
- [ ] What test preparation materials are available? (test samples, instructional materials, benchmark or other practice tests, etc.)
- [ ] What training is available at the school, district, state, and regional levels for teachers and parents?
- [ ] What are the implications and consequences of the test results for students, teachers, schools, and districts?
- [ ] Who composes the tests and what input may you have on their design?
- [ ] What local, state, regional, and national resources are available that address standardized testing? (organizations, educational boards and agencies, advocacy and research groups, professional and community Listservs, Web-based message boards, etc.)
- [ ] Whom can you contact at the school or district level for more information? (school dean of instruction, instructional specialist, department chairperson, other administrators, etc.)

The Information You Need: Resources for State Standards and Assessment

Much of the information for the checklist on page 7 is available from the resources below:

National Resources

No Child Left Behind Act Web site
http://www.ed.gov/nclb/landing.jhtml
> This Web site includes separate sections for students, parents, teachers, and administrators. It addresses testing, accountability, reading issues, teachers' roles, and much more. The site also provides links to an E-mail based subscription newsletter, details on policy and legislation, fact sheets, statistics and graphs, state testing information, and additional resources.

United States Department of Education
http://www.ed.gov/index.jhtml
> This site contains information for students, parents, teachers, and administrators on educational priorities, research and statistics, PreK–12 issues, as well as links to other educational resources.

National Education Association
http://www.nea.org/
> The NEA's site includes information on accountability and testing, help for parents, a legislative action center link, various publications, and current educational news.

Education News
http://www.educationnews.org/
> This Web site offers free, education-related information from all states, complete with daily headline stories and a searchable archive.

Teachvision.com
http://www.teachervision.fen.com/lesson-plans/lesson-10279.html
> This site provides an extensive list of resources on No Child Left Behind.

State Education Departments/Agencies

An asterisk (*) denotes a special Web site outlining standards/assessments if available.

Alabama Department of Education
50 North Ripley Street
P.O. Box 302101
Montgomery, AL 36104
Phone: (334) 242-9700
http://www.alsde.edu/html/home.asp

Alaska Department of Education and
    Early Development
801 West Tenth Street, Suite 200
Juneau, AK 99801-1878
Phone: (907) 465-2800
Fax: (907) 465-3452
http://www.educ.state.ak.us/home.html
* *http://www.educ.state.ak.us/standards/*
* *http://www.educ.state.ak.us/tls/assessment/*

Arizona Department of Education
1535 West Jefferson Street
Phoenix, AZ 85007
Phone: (602) 542-5393 or (800) 352-4558
http://www.ade.state.az.us/
* *http://www.ade.state.az.us/standards/*

Arkansas Department of Education
#4 Capitol Mall
Little Rock, AR 72201
Phone: (501) 682-4475
http://arkedu.state.ar.us/
* *http://arkedu.state.ar.us/actaap/index.htm*

California Department of Education
1430 N Street
Sacramento, CA 95814
Phone: (916) 319-0800
http://goldmine.cde.ca.gov/
* *http://goldmine.cde.ca.gov/statetests/*

Colorado Department of Education
201 East Colfax Avenue
Denver, CO 80203-1799
Phone: (303) 866-6600
Fax: (303) 830-0793
http://www.cde.state.co.us/index_home.htm
* *http://www.cde.state.co.us/index_stnd.htm*

Connecticut State Department of Education
165 Capitol Avenue
Hartford, CT 06145
Phone: (860) 713-6548
http://www.state.ct.us/sde/

Delaware Department of Education
401 Federal Street
P.O. Box 1402
Dover, DE 19903-1402
Phone: (302) 739-4601
Fax: (302) 739-4654
http://www.doe.state.de.us/index.htm
* *http://www.doe.state.de.us/AAB/*

Florida Department of Education
Office of the Commissioner
Turlington Building, Suite 1514
325 West Gaines Street
Tallahassee, FL 32399
Phone: (850) 245-0505
Fax: (850) 245-9667
http://www.fldoe.org/
* *http://www.firn.edu/doe/curric/prek12/*
   frame2.htm

Georgia Department of Education
2054 Twin Towers East
Atlanta, GA 30334
Phone: (404) 656-2800 or (800) 311-3627
Fax: (404) 651-6867
http://www.doe.k12.ga.us/index.asp
* Georgia Learning Connections Web site:
   http://www.glc.k12.ga.us/
   GLC Phone: (404) 651-5664
   GLC Fax: (404) 657-5183

Hawaii Department of Education
1390 Miller Street
P.O. Box 2360
Honolulu, HI 96804
Phone: (808) 586-3230
Fax: (808) 586-3234
http://doe.k12.hi.us/
* *http://doe.k12.hi.us/standards/index.htm*

Idaho Department of Education
650 West State Street
P.O. Box 83720
Boise, ID 83720-0027
Phone: (208) 332-6800
http://www.sde.state.id.us/Dept/
* *http://www.sde.state.id.us/admin/standards/*

Illinois State Board of Education
100 North First Street
Springfield, IL 62777-0001
Phone: (217) 782-4321 or (866) 262-6663
Fax: (217) 524-4928
TTY: (217) 782-1900
http://www.isbe.state.il.us/
* *http://www.isbe.state.il.us/ils/*

Indiana Department of Education
Room 229, State House
Indianapolis, IN 46204-2798
Phone: (317) 232-6610
Fax: (317) 232-8004
http://doe.state.in.us/welcome.html
* *http://doe.state.in.us/asap/welcome.html*

Iowa Department of Education
Grimes State Office Building
Des Moines, IA 50319-0146
Phone: (515) 281-5294
Fax: (515) 242-5988
http://www.state.ia.us/educate/index.html
* *http://www.state.ia.us/educate/ecese/nclb/doc/*
   ccsb.html

Kansas State Department of Education
120 SE Tenth Avenue
Topeka, KS 66612-1182
Phone: (785) 296-3201
Fax: (785) 296-7933
http://www.ksbe.state.ks.us/Welcome.html
* http://www.ksbe.state.ks.us/assessment/ index.html

Kentucky Department of Education
500 Mero Street
Frankfort, KY 40601
Phone: (502) 564-4770 or (800) 533-5372
TTY: (502) 564-4970
http://www.kde.state.ky.us/

Louisiana Department of Education
P.O. Box 94064
Baton Rouge, LA 70804-9064
Phone: (877) 453-2721
http://www.doe.state.la.us/
* http://www.doe.state.la.us/doecd/reaching.asp

Maine Department of Education
23 State House Station
Augusta, ME 04333-0023
Phone: (207) 624-6774
Fax: (207) 624-6771
http://www.state.me.us/education/
* http://www.state.me.us/education/lres/ homepage.htm

Maryland State Department of Education
200 West Baltimore Street
Baltimore, MD 21201
Phone: (410) 767-0100
http://marylandpublicschools.org/
* http://mdk12.org/

Massachusetts Department of Education
350 Main Street
Malden, MA 02148-5023
Phone: (781) 338-3000
http://www.doe.mass.edu/
* http://www.doe.mass.edu/frameworks/current.html

Michigan Department of Education
608 West Allegan
Lansing, MI 48933
Phone: (517) 373-3324
http://michigan.gov/mde/

Minnesota Department of Education
1500 Highway 36 West
Roseville, MN 55113-4266
Phone: (651) 582-8200
http://www.education.state.mn.us/html/mde_ home.htm

Mississippi Department of Education
Central High School
P.O. Box 771
359 North West Street
Jackson, MS 39205
Phone: (601) 359-3513
http://www.mde.k12.ms.us/
* http://marcopolo.mde.k12.ms.us/ frameworks.html

Missouri Department of Elementary and
  Secondary Education
P.O. Box 480
Jefferson City, MO 65102
Phone: (573) 751-4212
Fax: (573) 751-8613
http://www.dese.state.mo.us/
* http://www.dese.state.mo.us/standards/

Montana Office of Public Instruction
P.O. Box 202501
Helena, MT 59620-2501
Phone: (406) 444-3095 or (888) 231-9393
http://www.opi.state.mt.us/
* http://www.opi.state.mt.us/Standards/Index.html

Nebraska Department of Education
301 Centennial Mall South
Lincoln, NE 68509
Phone: (402) 471-2295
http://www.nde.state.ne.us/
* http://www.nde.state.ne.us/AcadStand.html

Nevada Department of Education
700 East Fifth Street
Carson City, NV 89701
Phone: (775) 687-9200
Fax: (775) 687-9101
http://www.nde.state.nv.us/
* *http://www.nde.state.nv.us/sca/standards/
  index.html*

New Hampshire Department of Education
101 Pleasant Street
Concord, NH 03301-3860
Phone: (603) 271-3494
Fax: (603) 271-1953
http://www.ed.state.nh.us/
* *http://www.ed.state.nh.us/Curriculum
  Frameworks/curricul.htm*

New Jersey Department of Education
P.O. Box 500
Trenton, NJ 08625
Phone: (609) 292-4469
http://www.state.nj.us/education/index.html
* *http://www.state.nj.us/njded/stass/index.html*

New Mexico Public Education Department
300 Don Gaspar
Santa Fe, NM 87501-2786
Phone: (505) 827-5800
http://www.sde.state.nm.us/
* *http://164.64.166.11/cilt/standards/*

New York State Education Department
89 Washington Avenue
Albany, NY 12234
http://www.nysed.gov/home.html
* *http://www.nysatl.nysed.gov/standards.html*

North Carolina Department of
   Public Instruction
301 North Wilmington Street
Raleigh, NC 27601
Phone: (919) 807-3300
http://www.ncpublicschools.org/
* *http://www.ncpublicschools.org/curriculum/*

North Dakota Department of
   Public Instruction
600 East Boulevard Avenue
Department 201
Floors 9, 10, and 11
Bismarck, ND 58505-0440
Phone: (701) 328-2260
Fax: (701) 328- 2461
http://www.dpi.state.nd.us/index.shtm
* *http://www.dpi.state.nd.us/standard/index.shtm*

Ohio Department of Education
25 South Front Street
Columbus, OH 43215-4183
Phone: (877) 644-6338
http://www.ode.state.oh.us/
* *http://www.ode.state.oh.us/academic_
  content_standards/*

Oklahoma State Department of Education
2500 North Lincoln Boulevard
Oklahoma City, OK 73105-4599
Phone: (405) 521-3301
Fax: (405) 521-6205
http://www.sde.state.ok.us/home/defaultie.html

Oregon Department of Education
255 Capitol Street NE
Salem, OR 97310-0203
Phone: (503) 378-3569
TDD: (503) 378-2892
Fax: (503) 378-5156
http://www.ode.state.or.us/
* *http://www.ode.state.or.us/asmt/standards/*

Pennsylvania Department of Education
333 Market Street
Harrisburg, PA 17126
Phone: (717) 783-6788
*http://www.pde.state.pa.us/pde_internet/site/
default.asp*
* *http://www.pde.state.pa.us/stateboard_ed/
  cwp/view.asp?a=3&Q=76716&stateboard_
  edNav=|5467|*

Rhode Island Department of Education
255 Westminster Street
Providence, RI 02903
Phone: (401) 222-4600
http://www.ridoe.net/
* *http://www.ridoe.net/standards/frameworks/
default.htm*

South Carolina Department of Education
1429 Senate Street
Columbia, SC 29201
Phone: (803) 734-8815
Fax: (803) 734-3389
http://www.myscschools.com/
* *http://www.myscschools.com/offices/cso/*

South Dakota Department of Education
700 Governors Drive
Pierre, SD 57501
http://www.state.sd.us/deca/Index.htm
* *http://www.state.sd.us/deca/OCTA/
contentstandards/index.htm*

Tennessee Department of Education
Andrew Johnson Tower, 6th Floor
Nashville, TN 37243-0375
Phone: (615) 741-2731
http://www.state.tn.us/education/
* *http://www.state.tn.us/education/ci/
cistandards.htm*

Texas Education Agency
1701 North Congress Avenue
Austin, TX 78701
Phone: (512) 463-9734
http://www.tea.state.tx.us/
* *http://www.tea.state.tx.us/teks/index.html*
* *http://www.tea.state.tx.us/student.assessment/
teachers.html*

Utah State Office of Education
250 East 500 South
P.O. Box 144200
Salt Lake City, UT 84114-4200
Phone: (801) 538-7500
http://www.usoe.k12.ut.us/
* *http://www.uen.org/core/*

Vermont Department of Education
120 State Street
Montpelier, VT 05620-2501
http://www.state.vt.us/educ/
* *http://www.state.vt.us/educ/new/html/pubs/
framework.html*

Virginia Department of Education
P.O. Box 2120
Richmond, VA 23218
Phone: (800) 292-3820
http://www.pen.k12.va.us/
* *http://www.pen.k12.va.us/VDOE/Instruction/
sol.html*

Washington Office of the Superintendent of
Public Instruction (OSPI)
Old Capitol Building
P.O. Box 47200
Olympia, WA 98504-7200
Phone: (360) 725-6000
TTY: (360) 664-3631
http://www.k12.wa.us/
* *http://www.k12.wa.us/curriculuminstruct/*

West Virginia Department of Education
1900 Kanawha Boulevard East
Charleston, WV 25305
Phone: (304) 558-3660
Fax: (304) 558-0198
http://wvde.state.wv.us/

Wisconsin Department of Public Instruction
125 South Webster Street
P.O. Box 7841
Madison, WI 53707-7841
Phone: (608) 266-3390 or (800) 441-4563
http://www.dpi.state.wi.us/index.html
* *http://www.dpi.state.wi.us/dpi/dlsis/
currinst.html*

Wyoming Department of Education
2300 Capitol Avenue
Hathaway Building, 2nd Floor
Cheyenne, WY 82002-0050
Phone: (307) 777-7675
Fax: (307) 777-6234
http://www.k12.wy.us/index.asp
* *http://www.k12.wy.us/eqa/nca/pubs/
standards.asp*

Introducing the Tests to Your Students

Before tackling any new task, it is a good idea to come up with a game plan for how to proceed. Figuring out a game plan and conveying it to your students can make the task of test taking seem more manageable and even fun!

This book outlines the steps for a game plan and gives you the tools you will need along the way, including innovative activities and sample test questions. However, the approach you use in preparing your students will be key to their success. This book's game plan is designed to draw upon your strengths as an encouraging and motivating teacher—in short, as a testing "coach."

Chapter 2 explains how to get students started on the right foot. It shows you how to present state standardized tests as important challenges students can train for as a team.

The Coach Approach

The activities in this book are designed to build upon and enhance skills that are assessed on state standardized tests, but in a way that is active, engaging, and fun. Since this is not your average drill-and-practice test-preparation workbook, you can be creative in your approach to working on these skills. Adopting the persona of coach can make all the difference in tackling the challenges your students face with these important tests. Using the coach approach can help eliminate test anxiety, build confidence, develop skills, and increase motivation.

Attitude Check

Coaching can be viewed as the application of teaching strategies to a set of activities that introduce, reinforce, and synthesize skills that players (students) need to perform their best. The role involves juggling many tasks at once. As a coach, you are an instructor, a facilitator, a motivator, a troubleshooter, and a supporter, all in one. The role also implies a strong desire to do the job and do it well.

Before developing your coach persona, it is crucial to evaluate how you feel about and approach standardized tests. A teacher's attitude and nonverbal messages can have a big impact on students, whether intentional or not. You may have quite a few legitimate gripes about the amount of time required for testing and preparation, the design of the tests, and the sometimes questionable uses of test scores. Regardless of these issues, take a moment to reflect on the following questions related to testing:

1. As a student, how did you feel about testing? Were you confident, careless, or anxious?
2. How do you feel about taking time from (or building time within) the curriculum to address test preparation?
3. How do you feel when testing results are published and available?
4. What can you do to make the testing process productive for you and your students?

Use your responses to these questions as the first steps in establishing your coaching character.

Putting On Your Game Face

As a good coach, you will motivate your students to perform their best, giving them the confidence to work on skills that need improvement. Coaching is a long-term process, requiring both dedication and flexibility. A successful coach will be:

- ✗   Patient
- ✗   Positive
- ✗   Motivated
- ✗   Resourceful
- ✗   Creative

Just as the students will work on skills where needed, so will you. As you regularly think about and use essential coaching skills, you will continue to gain confidence with them.

Suiting up as a coach does not mean shedding all of your qualities as a teacher. One way to help unite these two important roles is to evaluate how test preparation draws upon core teaching skills and instructional objectives. Since all state standardized tests are based on curriculum standards, look at the tests through the lens of authentic assessment. The tests are the outcomes of skills and content students are already learning rather than extraneous hurdles for students to overcome. Try to view test preparation as an opportunity to incorporate innovative strategies, diverse activities, and alternative approaches to content into your curriculum. This will allow you to prepare students for the tests without losing sight of the fundamentals of learning and quality instruction.

Use this perspective to develop a positive outlook toward the tests, and your attitude will be obvious to your students. To foster the same attitude among students, try to convey the importance of the tests to them—not just in terms of assessment, but also in terms of their development as learners. Describe both the purpose and outcomes of the tests in terms of what students will gain from them. Explain that the tests will help students focus their learning, shape up some of their academic skills, and give students opportunities to demonstrate what they have learned. Students will train for the tests like professional athletes training for a competition. On the big day, they will have a chance to demonstrate just how good they really are.

Synonymous with coaching is motivating. To get yourself in a motivational frame of mind, try to view the upcoming tests as academic challenges rather than obstacles. Transfer this energy to students by encouraging them to think of each test as a big game for which they are preparing. Try to develop a team spirit in the class. Talk about how you are going to give students the techniques, strategies, and experience they need to achieve peak performance. When introducing any of the activities provided in this book, explain exactly how each activity will make students better, stronger test-takers.

A resourceful coach is one who does not see limits, but rather possibilities or alternatives. If one strategy does not work, try something else or modify the strategy to meet the needs of your players. If some of the activities or strategies outlined in this book do not seem to "click" with students, let your creative sensibilities revise them to better suit your students' needs.

Devising a Game Plan

A good coach plans ahead in order to prepare the team for victory. After you have determined your individual approach to coaching, the next step is to develop a game plan. A successful game plan will include activities and exercises targeted to the particular needs of the team. By focusing on areas where students need a boost, you will help them evolve from a scrappy set of inexperienced players to an accomplished team of testing aces. Here is an overview of the instructional game plan outlined in this book:

X Assess students' abilities through a diagnostic test (Chapter 3).

X Set realistic goals for the team based on diagnostic results.

X Use goals to develop objectives for skill development.

X Break down skills into accessible segments by using specific math activities (Chapter 5).

X Involve the team in new approaches that use more than one skill at a time (Chapter 5).

X Simulate the game environment through test scrimmages and practice testing scenarios (Chapters 3 and 6).

X Incorporate strategies that help boost skills and performance (Chapter 4).

X Evaluate the process and teach students how to evaluate what they are doing (Chapter 4).

Before devising a training program, the coach must discern where the players are and where they need to go in order to be successful. That is why we recommend starting your program with the checklist and diagnostic test in Chapter 3. By first assessing your students' skills and their familiarity with the format of standardized tests, you will be able to formulate an appropriate and realistic plan to help them best prepare for the tests ahead. Using this plan, you can then select suitable activities to work on particular skills and present meaningful strategies for students to apply during the tests.

When introducing your state's math test to students, establish your role as coach from the beginning. Explain that you will be working with the students to figure out where they are in order to get them where they should be before the "big game." Make it clear that along the way, you will be showing them several strategies they can use in their weaker areas when they feel trapped with the ball, so to speak.

Describe the test not as something impossible to beat, but as something that students can handle on their own. The training program you are developing, based on the students' "pre-event trial" (the diagnostic test in Chapter 3) will help prepare them well for the test. Explain that you will also help them stay motivated and maintain a positive attitude toward the test throughout the program. Make it clear that you welcome any ideas they may have to make the process more fun and less tedious.

Cross Training in the Classroom

Since you want to avoid burnout that can happen through basic drill instruction, and since you are an innovative coach by nature, try cross training your academic athletes.

In the usual sense, cross training means varying a regular exercise routine with different forms of exercise to reach the same goal. For example, soccer players may lift weights, football players may take up ballet, and runners may try bicycling to vary their workouts. These different types of activities give athletes new strengths and skills that make them better at their primary sports.

Cross training is an important facet of the coaching philosophy. It can easily be applied to training your students to face testing challenges. Drilling students with practice questions is an important part of test preparation, but it can become monotonous and boring. Cross training can keep students from getting bored. If students are given a variety of methods for developing testing skills, they will learn to apply their skills in different contexts, adapt their strategies to different activities, and synthesize these skills and strategies more naturally when performing on tests. Chapters 4 and 5 of this book address methods of cross training and provide ways to change up the normal "training program" for your students. Here are a few suggestions taken from those chapters:

X   Intermingle straight drills with activities.

X   Use different or unusual content to teach skills that cross disciplines.
(For example, use a science article to teach students about statistical averages or a poem to teach about identifying patterns.)

X   Engage students in activities that practice and develop more than one skill at a time.

X   Weave into the training program methods students can use to deal with test anxiety.

X   Avoid overtraining by taking breaks. Plan "rest days" where the goal is to have fun learning something new or trying something different, rather than simply mastering another skill.

A beginning team may need to start with simple objectives before moving up to the goal of winning or beating the opponent. From this standpoint, building upon individual skills incrementally may be an approach you will want to try with your students. Having students exercise many skills at once can also keep tedium on the sidelines while encouraging a more integrated application that reflects the real world. This book provides some activities that focus on one particular standard or skill each, as well as others that tie related skills together in integrated ways.

The Mental Game: Motivation, Metacognition, and Modeling

One of the most important aspects of coaching is motivation. Motivated students have an edge when faced with any academic challenge. Give your students plenty of compelling reasons to want to do well on state tests and boost their self-confidence by preparing them thoroughly. If they want to do well for themselves and believe they can learn new skills, students will be well prepared and focused on testing days.

Coaching also involves constant evaluation—of progress, of problems, and of the process itself. Helping students develop metacognitive skills, or making them aware of their own processes and progress, will pay off enormously. Use the test-taking strategies in Chapter 4 to teach your students how to think about what they are doing while they are doing it and to identify their own strengths and weaknesses. Encourage them to use their minds to reduce anxiety and alleviate fears about testing. Using metacognition throughout the test-preparation process will help students stay focused and remain in control during the tests.

Another way to help students psych themselves up for testing is to model a positive attitude toward the process. Try not to let any frustrations you may have about the tests dampen your students' motivation. Encourage team spirit by talking about each test as a big game. Explain that you are going to prepare the students by giving them the techniques, strategies, and experiences needed to give a peak performance. And when introducing the activities in this book, describe exactly how they will help students become better, stronger test-takers.

Standardized tests are a fact a life for students today. Your job as a coach is to teach them how to tackle those tests with confidence. You can remove the often crippling obstacles of anxiety and uncertainty from your students' paths, but it will take some work. The activities, strategies, and sample tests in this book, coupled with your own persistence and creativity as a coach, will all work together to boost students' skills and confidence.

How Coaching Looks in the Classroom

Since coaching is an active and involved role, any instruction related to your state's standardized tests should be, too. The activities in this book reflect this hands-on approach and provide lots of modeling potential. Each activity has been broken down into the following categories, allowing you to guide students through it step-by-step: Skills/State Standards, Description, Materials You Need, Getting Ready, Introducing the Activity, Modeling the Activity, Activity in Practice, and Extensions.

The activities are designed for collaborative pair or group work. However, many are adaptable and can be used with individual students for more focused skill instruction. No matter how you decide to use them, the activities are student-centered in nature, allowing you, the coach, to facilitate and assess while students actively develop their skills.

Identifying Problem Areas

In order to develop a program that will bring your students to peak performance on state assessment tests, begin by identifying any problem areas in their skill development. This will save you time and energy in the long run, and make the whole experience of preparing for the tests more advantageous for students. The short math test in this chapter is representative of eighth-grade state assessment tests. You may use this test as a diagnostic tool. But before administering the test, determine what exposure your students already have to the look, feel, and content of your state's tests. Think about what they do in the classroom that addresses test preparation in some way. Since your state's standards serve as the scaffolding for the curriculum, students should already be learning the content and developing the skills that will be assessed on the tests. However, they may not realize that what they are learning directly connects to the tests they will take. Use the following checklist of questions to review your students' current testing knowledge.

Checklist: Evaluating Your Students' Testing Savvy

General Questions

- ☐ Do students have experience with multiple-choice tests?
- ☐ How often do students take tests individually?
- ☐ What forms of standardized tests have students taken this year or previously?
- ☐ Do students have frequent practice using answer sheets to record their answers?

Math Questions

- ☐ How familiar are students with basic algebraic concepts and operations?
- ☐ How often do students use geometric terms, operations, and models?
- ☐ How often do students use measurement to determine area, develop formulas, and estimate answers?
- ☐ How often do students apply different number theories and operations depending on the context?
- ☐ How often do students use calculators to perform more complex operations?
- ☐ How often do students create, interpret, analyze, and evaluate graphic representations?
- ☐ How often do students identify mean, median, mode, and range?
- ☐ How often do students use formulas or equations to solve word problems?
- ☐ How often do students match ratios, equations, or expressions with written descriptions?
- ☐ Do students round numbers when estimating?
- ☐ Can students use information given in sequence to determine patterns or identify missing information?
- ☐ Do students know how to use deductive and inductive reasoning to solve problems?

For a tailor-made checklist based on your state's standards, use the information provided by your state's education department or agency on the math standards for grade eight. (See Chapter 1, pages 8–12.)

Diagnostic Math Test—Grade 8

Directions: This test contains 18 problems. Read and solve each problem. Mark your answers on your answer sheet. Be sure to fill in each bubble completely and erase any stray marks.

1 Which property does the equation below demonstrate?

$$24 \times (21 \times 12) = (24 \times 21) \times 12$$

 A associative

B commutative

C distributive

D identity

2 Mr. Greco took out a loan at an annual interest rate of 6.7%. He paid off the loan in 12 months. Which expression can be used to find the total interest he paid, if p is the principal?

F $p - 0.067 \times 1$

G $p \times 0.067 \div 12$

H $p \times 0.067 \times 1$

J $p \times 0.067 \times 12$

3 The distance between Jupiter and the sun is about 4.836×10^8 miles. How would you write this distance in standard form?

A 4,836,000 miles

B 48,360,000 miles

C 483,600,000 miles

D 4,836,000,000 miles

4 A computer salesperson earned a commission of $175 on the sale of a $2,500 computer system. Which statement below identifies a commission that is at the same rate?

F A commission of $210 on the sale of a $3000 computer system

G A commission of $325 on the sale of a $3,500 computer system

H A commission of $500 on the sale of a $4,000 computer system

J A commission of $550 on the sale of a $4,500 computer system

GO ON

5 The grid below represents the top view of a solid figure made of stacked cubes. The number in each square identifies the number of cubes in each stack.

3	4	3
2	4	1
1	2	1

Front

Which drawing below shows a three-dimensional view of the figure represented by the grid?

A

B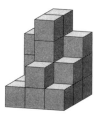

C

D

6 Clara made a curtain for a window to keep out the sun. The dimensions of the area enclosed by the window are shown in the diagram below.

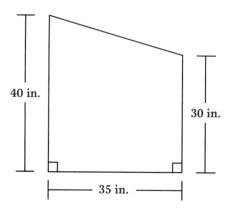

What is the total area, in square inches, of Clara's curtain?

F 1,050 in.²

G 1,200 in.²

H 1,225 in.²

J 1,400 in.²

GO ON

Name: **Date:**

Diagnostic Math Test—Grade 8 (continued)

7 Heloise is making a color grid for a game. Each player in the game tries to land a cube in a certain square on the grid. Heloise needs to write a color in the shaded square to complete the grid.

yellow	purple		blue
green	blue	yellow	purple
purple	green	blue	yellow

What color should Heloise write in the shaded square so that the probability of landing the cube on that color is $1/4$?

A yellow

B green

C blue

D purple

8 Which equation identifies the pattern shown in this table?

m	5	8	12	16
n	30	42	58	74

F $n = m^2 + 5$

G $n = 2m + 5$

H $n = 4m + 10$

J $n = m^3 - 12$

9 Casey is in charge of distributing spirit ribbons to student council members to sell for their fund-raiser. Each box of 150 ribbons costs $25. The student council purchases 10 boxes. If the ribbons are sold for 25¢ each, how many ribbons does the council need to sell before they make a profit?

A 250 ribbons

B 500 ribbons

C 1,000 ribbons

D 1,500 ribbons

GO ON

10   The table below lists the finish times of seven swimmers in a district swim competition.

What time represents the mode?

Swim Times

Lane Number	Time (min.sec)
1	1.35
2	1.34
3	1.27
4	1.34
5	1.28
6	1.30
7	1.31

Record your answer in the bubble grid below and on your answer sheet. Write your answer across the top and fill in the corresponding bubbles in each column.

11   A billboard sign is 20 feet tall. The wooden braces behind the sign are 25 feet long.

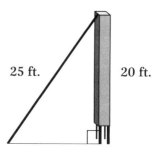

25 ft.   20 ft.

What is the distance from the base of the billboard sign to the bottom of the wooden braces?

F   8 ft.

G   10 ft.

H   15 ft.

J   18 ft.

12   A car traveling at a certain speed will travel 96 feet per second. How many yards will the car travel in 120 seconds if it maintains that same speed?

A   94 yards

B   376 yards

C   3,840 yards

D   11,280 yards

Diagnostic Math Test—Grade 8 (continued)

13   The table below shows the number of pages in 24 paperback books in different categories.

Lengths of Paperback Books

Category			
Adventure	Suspense	Science Fiction	Fantasy
110 pages	64 pages	90 pages	85 pages
118 pages	84 pages	115 pages	109 pages
92 pages	85 pages	105 pages	120 pages
95 pages	74 pages	75 pages	95 pages
113 pages	90 pages	100 pages	100 pages
104 pages	82 pages	80 pages	90 pages

Which histogram best represents the information in the chart?

F

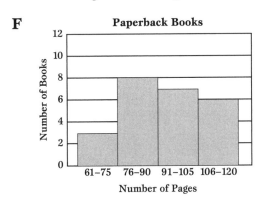

G

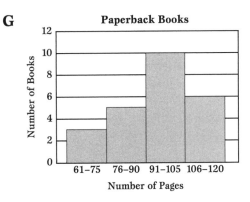

H

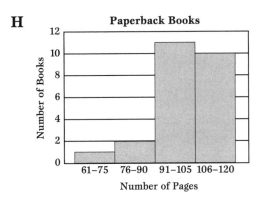

J

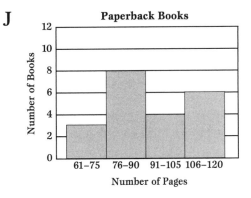

GO ON

Diagnostic Math Test—Grade 8 (continued)

14 Tasha saves a portion of the money she makes at her after-school job in a savings account. The savings account earns 2% interest. Tasha is saving up to buy a stereo system that costs $1,500 plus tax. Sales tax is 8%. Tasha wants to buy the system in 6 months and has already saved a third of the amount she will need.

What other information is necessary to determine how much money Tasha still needs to save?

A the amount of money she saves each month

B the amount of money in her savings account

C the type of stereo system she wants to buy

D the payment plan offered by the stereo store

15 Organic tomatoes are on sale for $2.99 per pound. Each tomato weighs about one-fifth of a pound. What is the BEST estimate for the cost of 50 tomatoes?

F $30

G $35

H $45

J $50

16 The volume of the rectangular solid below is 1,728 cubic inches.

6 in.

What could be the length and width of this rectangular solid?

A 30 in. × 8 in.

B 16 in. × 10 in.

C 24 in. × 12 in.

D 28 in. × 8 in.

GO ON

17 Nadine decides to spend her allowance on three pairs of shoes. The first pair costs $25.99, the second pair costs $21.99, and the third pair costs $27.99. If she pays 7% sales tax, what is the total amount of her purchase?

Record your answer in the bubble grid below and on your answer sheet. Write your answer across the top and fill in the corresponding bubbles in each column.

18 The width of the rectangle below is represented by a certain positive number z. Its length is represented by the expression $z + 4$.

$$z \quad \boxed{}$$
$$z + 4$$

Which expression represents the area of the rectangle?

F $2z + (z + 4)$

G $2z + 2(z + 4)$

H $z + (z + 4)$

J $z(z + 4)$

STOP

END OF PRACTICE TEST

Diagnostic Math Test—Grade 8
Answer Sheet

Directions: Mark your answers on this answer sheet. Be sure to fill in each bubble completely and erase any stray marks.

1 Ⓐ Ⓑ Ⓒ Ⓓ

2 Ⓕ Ⓖ Ⓗ Ⓙ

3 Ⓐ Ⓑ Ⓒ Ⓓ

4 Ⓕ Ⓖ Ⓗ Ⓙ

5 Ⓐ Ⓑ Ⓒ Ⓓ

6 Ⓕ Ⓖ Ⓗ Ⓙ

7 Ⓐ Ⓑ Ⓒ Ⓓ

8 Ⓕ Ⓖ Ⓗ Ⓙ

9 Ⓐ Ⓑ Ⓒ Ⓓ

10 Write your answer across the top of the bubble grid. Fill in the corresponding bubbles in each column.

11 Ⓕ Ⓖ Ⓗ Ⓙ

12 Ⓐ Ⓑ Ⓒ Ⓓ

13 Ⓕ Ⓖ Ⓗ Ⓙ

14 Ⓐ Ⓑ Ⓒ Ⓓ

15 Ⓕ Ⓖ Ⓗ Ⓙ

16 Ⓐ Ⓑ Ⓒ Ⓓ

17 Write your answer across the top of the bubble grid. Fill in the corresponding bubbles in each column.

18 Ⓕ Ⓖ Ⓗ Ⓙ

Test-Taking Skills and Strategies

When preparing for a test, students don't normally prepare for *how* to take the test. They are usually more worried about what they do or do not know than about how their approach can affect their performance. And with the added pressure of these high-stakes assessment tests, the concept of strategic test taking may be the last thing on their minds.

Your role as coach is twofold: to help your students do well on the tests, and to equip them with strategies they can use to refuel, relax, or refocus in order to reach the finish line. This chapter outlines several strategies students can learn to deal with problems that may surface when taking tests.

Getting students into the right frame of mind for testing is one of the most challenging tasks facing a coach. This chapter addresses the most common issues involving testing, and offers both you and your students ways to incorporate test-taking skills and strategies into the framework of test preparation. The chapter is broken down into the following sections:

- X Reducing Test Anxiety
- X Pacing
- X Strategic Guessing
- X Math Strategies
- X Top Five Test-Taking Tips for Students

Some activities have accompanying reproducible handouts for students to use during the activity. These reproducible pages are arranged by strategy beginning on page 36. Ideas for additional practice or related activities are labeled as "Coaching Clues" and appear throughout this chapter.

Reducing Test Anxiety

When faced with standardized tests, students may experience a range of reactions, one of the most unsettling being anxiety. To help students replace test anxiety with test confidence, talk about the tests, familiarize students with the test format and structure, and give them techniques to deal with any stress or distractions that may occur during testing.

You may want to begin by asking students to reflect on their own attitudes toward test taking. Discuss the different feelings the prospect of taking a test may arouse, as well as how students might deal with those feelings. Also, discuss any strategies students may already be using when they take tests.

> ***Coaching Clue*** — Using the *Testing Questionnaire* reproducible (page 36) as a starting point, encourage students to discuss and reflect on the testing process.

The more familiar students are with the tests they will take, the less stress they will likely experience. One way to help reduce test anxiety is to make students so familiar with the test format that they don't even flinch when faced with the actual tests. Pages 28 and 29 include several ways to familiarize students with your state's assessment tests.

Break It Down

Take a sample, benchmark, or previously released test developed by your state's education department and break it down for analysis. Divide the class into small groups and ask each group to analyze the format, content, language, and style of the test. Once all of the groups have completed their analyses and shared their findings, review the major points about each aspect of the test. Make a chart or poster to display as a classroom reference.

> **Coaching Clue** — Use the *Meet Your Math Test* reproducible (page 37) to try out this break-it-down strategy. Students can use the questions on the handout as a guide in their analysis and discussion.

Be a Copycat

Design assignments, quizzes, and tests in the same layout and format as your state's tests. If your state's math test uses a particular numbering font or the graphics are done in a distinctive style, try to replicate that on any quizzes or assignments you create based on your curriculum.

Test Experts

Have students write sample questions in the same format as your state's tests, based on math concepts they are learning in class. Have students test one another using their sample questions.

Tip Trade

Students may already have some tricks up their sleeves when it comes to dealing with testing issues. Before the test time, brainstorm together different tricks or hints students have for dealing with stress, pacing, guessing, or other test-taking issues. Then, have them teach these skills to one another in small groups or to the entire class. As a follow-up, give them the opportunity to practice these new skills either with practice tests or tests written by the students themselves. (See "Test Experts" above.)

Make It Real

Common sense tells us that the more preparation we have before attempting something, the better we will do. In the same vein, testing experts state that the more exposure students have to the look, feel, and experience of tests before testing day, the better they will perform.

With this in mind, give students an authentic simulation of the testing experience at least once before the actual tests. You could use the sample tests included in Chapters 3 and 6, or sample tests from your state's education department. Alternatively, design your own test with the look and feel of your state's tests, but based on recent coursework learned by the students. Although you don't want to reach testing overload with students, you do want to give them opportunities to apply what they have learned. Creating authentic test simulations can help you and your students work out any kinks in the process while strengthening students' skills and building their confidence.

Some schools even hold simulation days when students throughout the school take a benchmark or trial test. Use these simulations to promote discussion with your students about their test-taking experiences. Make sure students realize that a low score on a practice test is nothing to get worried or upset about. Instead, a low score should be seen as an excellent way to spot what areas need to be improved on before the real test.

Coaching Clue — After students have taken some practice quizzes and tests, have them analyze their test-taking experiences. Use the *Talking It Over* reproducible (page 38) as a guide for this activity.

Pacing

While the majority of state standardized tests are timed, your own state's tests may not be. But regardless of time limits, pacing can play a key role in a student's testing success. Pacing can help students stay on track by helping them focus their concentration, maintain their stamina, and offset any anxiety.

To introduce the concept of pacing, have students envision the tests as a series of track-and-field events. Each part of the test is like a different event. Even if students want to get the best time or highest score for one event, pacing their energy and concentration among all the events they face will ensure a better result overall. Have them practice and employ the following strategies to bolster their endurance and even out their tempo during testing.

X-O Strategy

A steady pace ensures the best performance. However, sometimes a student will come across a question that stumps him, causing him to lose his sense of rhythm. Most students approach questions as if they have to be done in order. When they hit hard questions, they get stuck and refuse to move on. And the longer they stay stuck, the more anxious and frustrated they become. This is a strategic mistake. Students' scores and attitudes will both get a boost if they make two or three passes through a test, each time skipping questions that seem too hard and going back to them after they have tried to answer all of the other questions.

The X-O strategy is a simple way to maintain a good pace and maximize scores. When working through a section, a student should first take the time to solve or answer any questions she can. However, if she starts to struggle with a confusing problem and spends more than a few minutes on it without coming up with an answer, she should stop and mark an "X" in the margin next to the question. This is a "maybe" question. The student could probably figure out the solution if she spent some more time, but for now she needs to move on and try to answer other easier problems.

If the student comes to a question that initially makes no sense to her at all, she should mark an "O" in the margin. This is a "guessing" question. Using strategic guessing techniques can help improve the odds of the student selecting the correct answer on this type of question.

After the student has answered every question she can, she should return to the X questions first and try them again. If they still give her trouble, she should apply strategic guessing techniques, such as process of elimination (discussed on pages 32–33), to eliminate any incorrect answers. Once some of the possible answers have been eliminated, the student can make an educated guess. After the student has tried to answer all of the X questions, she should go back to the O questions and apply the same strategic guessing techniques.

The X-O strategy keeps students from freezing up when faced with tough questions. It also encourages them to answer every question, which will ultimately help their scores.

Coaching Clue — For practice using the X-O strategy with students, see the *X-O Strategy* reproducible (page 39) at the end of this chapter.

Time-Outs

Most experts believe that the average person can only handle 45 minutes of learning new material before reaching complete absorption. This belief is the reasoning behind the "45/15" rule: after 45 minutes of study, take a 15-minute break. If this is a good method for students to use when studying, why not apply it, in a modified form, to taking a test? Tell students that one way to pace themselves during a test is to take a time-out after each section. Alternatively, they can take a break every half hour or so, stretching a bit while still at their desks. Encourage students to use the timed breaks to get up and stretch, get a drink of water, or walk around the hall a bit to refresh themselves before going back to the test.

Desk Stretches

Most state assessment tests are several hours long. Students understandably find it difficult and uncomfortable to remain in the same position for a very long time. To help students combat desk fatigue, teach them some stretches they can do while sitting at their desks. The exercises that follow on page 31 are written so you can read them directly from the page to your students.

Four-Square Neck Stretches

1. Sitting straight in your chair, tilt your head forward, trying to touch your chin to your chest. Hold for five counts.

2. Tilt your head backward and look up at the ceiling, letting the back of your head rest on the base of your neck while keeping your shoulders relaxed. Hold for five counts.

3. Tilt your head to the right, so your ear is close to your right shoulder. Hold for five counts.

4. Tilt your head to the left, so your ear is close to your left shoulder. Hold for five counts.

Shoulder Roll and Pull

1. While seated at your desk, roll both shoulders forward in a circular motion. Continue for a count of ten. Try to keep your neck relaxed while you roll, concentrating on rotating the shoulders in circles rather than just lifting them straight up and down.

2. Switch direction and roll your shoulders backward, also for a count of ten.

3. Next, clasp your hands together and extend your arms out from your chest, as if you are getting ready to hit a volleyball with your forearms. Concentrate on separating your shoulder blades, pulling the muscles in your upper back away from the center and out toward your hands. Hold for five counts.

Answer Bubbles

All standardized tests require students to record their answers by filling in some form of lettered bubbles. As with anything else, the more experience students have using bubble answer sheets, the more natural the process will be during the actual tests. Give students the practice they need by incorporating bubble-style answer grids into everyday activities, from daily warm-ups to homework review or pop quizzes.

One of the pitfalls of skipping a question in the test booklet is that a student may forget to skip that problem on the answer sheet. Having students use simple bookmarks or rulers while testing can help them stay on top of which problems they are skipping and need to go back to later. Check your state's guidelines to see if tools like these are allowed during testing.

Another approach is to have students record their choices on the answer sheet after they have finished each section. This reduces the risk of filling in the bubbles incorrectly. Just tell students to write or circle their final answer choice for each question in the test booklet itself. Then, after each section, they can transfer their answers to the answer sheet.

Coaching Clue — To give students extra practice, provide bubble grids similar to those on your state's tests for students to use with short quizzes or other classroom assignments.

Strategic Guessing

Even though state assessment exams do not normally feature a guessing penalty, this does not mean students should just guess randomly. Encourage students to use strategic guessing strategies by explaining how this can help them choose smart answers and in turn raise their scores.

Make it clear to your students from the start that guessing is not cheating. If they think they don't know what could possibly be the right answer, remind them that they have multiple tools on hand for every question. They can use prior knowledge and experience as well as what they just learned by reading a passage or thinking about a problem. These tools, combined with smart guessing, can all help a student figure out what the correct answer might be.

Although the X-O strategy (pages 29–30) can help students pace themselves throughout the test, it can also be used as the first step toward guessing strategically. If students begin by answering the questions they definitely know first, they can then go back and deal with the remaining questions using smart guessing and the process of elimination.

POE: Process of Elimination

Applying POE, or the process of elimination, during a test simply means weeding out any unsuitable answer choices. The inherent beauty of multiple-choice tests is that the correct answers are always provided—students just have to learn how to identify them.

Students are often amazed and encouraged when you explain that the right answers are in plain view in their test booklets. To get students comfortable with POE, first explain that the answers are all there on the page. Then, show them how the process works. Write a sample question, such as the following, on the board or on an overhead transparency:

How high is Mount Everest?

A	528 ft.
B	29,035 ft.
C	1,263,328 ft.
D	1,480 ft.

Tell your students that with some basic knowledge, good estimations, and common sense, they can reason through this question. Help them work through the POE process. First, talk about Mount Everest. What is it? A really tall mountain. What else do they know about it? They might know that people try to climb it but don't always succeed, even after many days of trying. This should give students some idea of the distance from the foot of the mountain to its peak. Now, help your students generate some lengths and heights to use for reference. For example, how long is a football field? Many students will know that a football field is 100 yards long, which is 300 feet. And how long is a mile? Some students will know this, too—5,280 feet. Ask them to think about how high a mountain might be, and then consider the answer choices.

- Choice A (528 feet) is less than twice the length of a football field. It would hardly be the height of a respectable mountain. Choice A can be eliminated.

- Choice B (29,035 feet) sounds like a lot. That would be about six miles of mountain. Choice B could be right, but keep going.
- Choice C (1,263,328 feet) sounds impressive, but does it make sense? A mountain that high would be about 240 miles tall. Many states aren't even 240 miles wide. Mountains just aren't that tall.
- Choice D (1,480 feet), like Choice A, does not seem tall enough. It is less than one mile. That just leaves Choice B, which is correct.

Point out to students that even though they did not actually know the height of Mount Everest, they were able to make a good guess by eliminating obviously wrong answers. This kind of reasoning can be applied to many standardized test questions with excellent results.

Coaching Clue — To try this as an exercise with students, tailor the steps outlined above to address a sample problem from one of your state's practice tests.

Critical Words and POE

As they apply the steps of POE, advise students to look for any critical (or extreme) words in the questions or answer choices. These words, which are often underlined, italicized, bold-faced, or set in all caps, may help students narrow down their choices or guide them in the right direction. Have them circle or underline any extreme words, such as:

NEVER	ONLY	ANY
EXCEPT	BEST	ALL
ALWAYS	NOT	NONE

Explain how these words can help students eliminate answer choices when common sense and prior experience are not helping. Very often, though not always, answer choices with critical or extreme words in them are wrong. If a student is forced to guess, you can advise her to cross out choices that involve critical or extreme words.

Flip a Coin

If a student has narrowed down the answer options as much as possible by eliminating wrong or unlikely choices, but he still has two or three possible answers, he should just pick an answer—guess and move on. The odds are that over the course of the test he will guess correctly at least some of the time, thus improving his score. Random guessing should be discouraged because it gives students the feeling that they can just give up and guess on hard questions when, in fact, some POE and deductive reasoning could help them get close to the right answer. The fact is, unless there is a guessing penalty on your state's test, students have nothing to lose by guessing. Tell them to answer every question but to guess blindly only if they have exhausted all of their smart guessing strategies.

Math Strategies

Word problems can present a real challenge for some students. Not only do they have to understand how to do the math, they must also figure out how to translate the words into mathematical equations to solve before they can even begin to answer the questions. This section offers several problem-solving strategies students can use to help them turn words into numbers in order to find a solution.

Draw It Out

Word problems often contain lots of details that can clutter students' minds as they try to find solutions. The Draw It Out strategy can help students by playing upon the visual nature of word problems. Applying this strategy, students draw or sketch out parts of the problem in order to clear up any confusion. This helps them visualize what is happening and allows them to use their own graphical representations to work towards solving the problem.

Coaching Clue — Use the *Draw It Out* reproducible (page 40) to guide students through a sample problem and show them how to apply this strategy.

Words That Reveal Mathematical Operations

Certain words that appear in word problems can indicate particular mathematical operations. Take a close look with your students at several sample word problems taken from class assignments or practice tests. Ask the students to try and pick out the key words or phrases in each problem that indicate how they might find the solution. Discuss what operation each word or phrase indicates.

Coaching Clue — The *Math Vocabulary Chart* reproducible (page 41) shows words and phrases that indicate particular mathematical operations. Make photocopies of this page for students to use as reference. In the additional space on the chart, have students add any other key words or phrases they may come across in their assignments or on tests.

Practice Makes Perfect

To help students make the transition from learning math concepts and skills in isolation to seeing math in real-world contexts, try to incorporate words and writing about math throughout the curriculum. Give students lots of practice by having them describe a problem-solving process using words rather than numbers, keep a learning log of processes, or translate number sentences into word-based relationships.

RIDDOTS *Strategy*

Once they have become fluent word-problem translators, teach students the RIDDOTS strategy. The simple acronym makes this strategy easy for students to remember and apply when taking a test on their own. RIDDOTS is an abbreviation for the following process:

Read the entire problem carefully.
IDentify any key words that will help you solve the problem.
Determine what you need to find out.
Omit any unnecessary details.
Translate the words into an equation.
Solve the equation and choose an answer.

Coaching Clue — Model the application of this strategy using the *RIDDOTS Strategy* reproducible (page 42) along with a variety of word problems like those that students are likely to see on your state's standardized tests.

Top Five Test-Taking Tips for Students

Finally, give students these five tips to remember before, during, and after the test. You may want to enlarge this list, or rewrite it in your own words and post the list in the room where students will take their tests.

1. **Be confident!**
   Remember that you are prepped to do well. You have been "working out" to get ready for the tests and can succeed. It's time to show what you can do.

2. **Be prepared!**
   Get a good night's sleep, eat a hearty breakfast, and wear clothes suitable for testing— comfortable layers you can take off or put on in case the testing room is too hot or cold. Bring all of the materials you will need, such as pencils, scratch paper, and a calculator.

3. **Review the test before you begin.**
   Before you start, spend a few minutes reviewing the test carefully. Familiarize yourself with each section and then decide how to pace yourself.

4. **Be focused and relaxed.**
   To keep up your concentration, use the test-taking strategies you have learned. If you begin to feel tense, take a few deep breaths and do some stretches.

5. **Look over the test when you are finished.**
   Make sure you have not skipped any sections and that you have answered every question. Check your answer sheet to make sure the bubbles are filled in neatly and correctly. Be sure to label your answers as needed.

Testing Questionnaire

Directions: Read each statement. Mark your answer by checking the appropriate box.

ALWAYS	SOME OF THE TIME	NEVER		
☐	☐	☐	1.	When I take a test, I feel confident that I am prepared and will do well.
☐	☐	☐	2.	The night before a test, I get a good night's sleep.
☐	☐	☐	3.	The morning before a test, I eat a good breakfast.
☐	☐	☐	4.	During a test, I feel my mind racing.
☐	☐	☐	5.	During a test, I feel alert and clearheaded.
☐	☐	☐	6.	When taking a test, I forget what I have learned and then remember it after I'm finished.
☐	☐	☐	7.	I make careless mistakes when taking a test.
☐	☐	☐	8.	I check my work and my answers before I turn in a test.
☐	☐	☐	9.	I rush to finish when I take a test.
☐	☐	☐	10.	When taking a test, I overanalyze questions, change my answers a lot, or don't answer at all.
☐	☐	☐	11.	If I don't know an answer, I narrow down my choices and take a guess.
☐	☐	☐	12.	If I don't know an answer, I skip it and come back to it later.
☐	☐	☐	13.	During a test, my breathing gets weird or my body feels tense.
☐	☐	☐	14.	If I don't understand a question or what I'm supposed to do on a test, I ask for help.
☐	☐	☐	15.	I lose concentration and am easily distracted by other people when taking a test.

Directions: Discuss your answers for numbers 1–15 with the rest of the class. Then, read each statement below. Mark your answer by checking the box for TRUE or FALSE.

☐ TRUE ☐ FALSE   16. It is better to guess on a question than to leave it blank.

☐ TRUE ☐ FALSE   17. Being the first one to finish a test is better than being the last one.

☐ TRUE ☐ FALSE   18. If you get bored or can't concentrate, you should just put your head down and go to sleep.

☐ TRUE ☐ FALSE   19. It's a waste of time to check your work before turning in a test.

☐ TRUE ☐ FALSE   20. You should never take a break during a test.

Meet Your Math Test

Directions: Together with your group, analyze your state's math test. Answer the questions below, writing your answers on the lines provided. Use a separate sheet of paper if needed. Be prepared to share your findings with the rest of the class.

1. What are some of the general directions you see throughout the test? _____

    _____

    _____

2. Is there a math reference sheet or chart included in the test booklet? _____

3. What kinds of tools are you allowed to use during the test (calculator, ruler, etc.)?

    _____

4. What types of problems are included on the test (basic geometry, algebraic equations, measurement, probability/statistics, percents/fractions, etc.)?

    _____

    _____

5. How many problems are there in all? _____

6. What types of responses are required (multiple choice, short answer, etc.)? _____

    _____

7. Is there space in the test booklet to work through the problems? _____

8. What types of graphics are included? How do these graphics relate to the problems?

    _____

    _____

9. Looking at the problems, which ones seem the hardest? Which ones seem the easiest?

    _____

    _____

10. After analyzing the problems, what do you think you need to do to prepare for the test?

    _____

    _____

Talking It Over

Directions: Answer the questions in the chart below. Use these questions as a starting point to discuss your testing experiences.

Reflecting on the Tests	
What did you find the **most challenging** about the tests?	What **techniques or strategies** did you use during the tests?

Preparing for the Real Thing
List the **major skills you want to work on** as you prepare for the state math test.

X-O Strategy

Directions: Use the X-O strategy to guide you through the test-taking process. Be sure to mark your test as instructed below and to complete all portions of this handout.

Round 1: Read through the questions or problems on the test. As you read, solve the problems you can answer without too much effort or time. Mark those answers on your answer sheet.

A. Mark an X by each problem that you think you can answer but are not sure about. Record the number of questions marked with an X here: _____

B. Mark an O by each problem for which you would have to guess the answer. Record the number of questions marked with an O here: _____

Round 2: Go back through the test and try to answer all of the questions marked with an X.

A. If you need to, reread, rework, or review the problems. Look for additional information to help you clarify anything or support the answers you think are correct.

B. Mark your answers on your answer sheet.

Round 3: Go back through the test and try to answer all of the questions marked with an O.

A. Note any critical words in the questions. Circle or underline these words and write them on the following lines.

_____

_____

B. Apply POE, or the process of elimination.

- Use common sense and logical reasoning to eliminate bad or unlikely answer choices. Think about how any critical words can help you determine the answers by eliminating some of the answer choices.

- Cross out any answer choices that you know are incorrect or unlikely.

- Try to narrow down the answer choices to two per problem.

C. Use your own prior knowledge, information from the problems, or any other clues given (such as graphs or illustrations) to make educated guesses. Mark your answers on your answer sheet.

Draw It Out

Directions: Use this handout as a guide when visualizing a word problem in order to solve it.

1. Write the word problem in the box below.

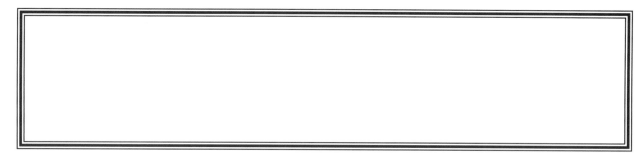

2. Underline or circle key words in the problem, and write them on the lines provided.

    _____   _____   _____

    _____   _____   _____

    _____   _____   _____

3. Use the space below to draw or sketch out the problem. Include the key words in your sketch. You can make one sketch or a series of sketches, depending on the word problem.

4. Based on the key words and your sketches, what is the problem asking you to find?

    _____

5. Use your sketches to help you solve the problem. Show your work on the back of this sheet, and then write your answer on the line below.

    _____

Math Vocabulary Chart

Meaning	Words and Phrases That Indicate Mathematical Operations		
Add ✚	increased by added to altogether	more than sum	total of combined
Subtract ▬	decreased by fewer than	minus less than	less difference between/of
Multiply ✖	times product of	multiplied by	increased by a factor of
Divide ➗	per ratio of	out of quotient of	percent (divide by 100)
Equals ═	is/are will be yields	was/were gives sold for	is equal to is the same as

RIDDOTS Strategy

Directions: Follow the steps to apply the RIDDOTS strategy to a sample word problem.

> Write a word problem in this space:

Follow the steps as listed in the left column to complete the boxes in the right column.

Read the entire problem carefully.	
IDentify any key words in the problem and write them in the box to the right.	
Determine what you need to find out: What are you trying to solve? What are you looking for?	
Omit unnecessary details from the word problem.	*Draw lines through words in the problem above that are NOT related to what you need to know or find out.*
Translate the words of the problem into an equation, formula, or mathematical expression.	
Solve the problem. • Show your work. (Use the back of this sheet if needed.) • Choose an answer, if provided. • Write your answer in the box to the right.	

Skill-Building Math Activities

This chapter includes 13 different activities designed to help you build and reinforce your students' mathematical skills. Each activity provides a fun way for students to practice one or more key skills that will be assessed on your state's standardized tests. The activities draw upon students' imaginations, experiences, and knowledge of the world around them while also strengthening their abilities to use math more frequently and fluidly. Each activity is structured in the following format:

✗ Skills/State Standards—breakdown of the skills addressed in the activity

✗ Description—brief summary of the activity

✗ Materials You Need—list of materials required for the activity

✗ Getting Ready—tips for the teacher and a description of what to do in order to prepare for the activity

✗ Introducing the Activity—suggestions for introducing the activity and capturing students' interest

✗ Modeling the Activity—ideas for demonstrating the activity (if applicable)

✗ Activity in Practice—step-by-step instructions for working through the activity

✗ Extensions—variations, extensions, and other teaching suggestions

The activities are designed to be hands-on and group-oriented, requiring active participation by your students. However, they are also flexible in nature and can be modified to meet your students' needs, as well as give students individual practice. You can use the activities in any order. You may find that some activities are more suited to the particular needs of your students than others.

Some activities also include reproducible materials or handouts. These reproducible pages are found at the end of this chapter, beginning on page 72.

The matrix on pages 44 and 45 organizes the activities by the predominant skills or standards they address. Some activities address more than one skill and may, therefore, appear under more than one category on the chart.

Matrix of Skills Addressed in Math Activities

Skill/State Standard	Activity	Page
Numbers and their operations	On Vacation.................................50 Newspaper Math.........................52 Backward Word Problems 64	
Algebraic equations, formulas, and applications	Show Me the Money ....46 Design a Zoo ....54 Backward Word Problems 64	
Mathematical and algebraic reasoning	Design a Zoo ....54 Backward Word Problems ....64 Mock Math Election ....66 What's Your Problem?................70	
Calculating percentages, fractions, and decimals	Show Me the Money ....46 Food for Thought......................48 On Vacation.................................50 Newspaper Math.........................52 Wall Street 68	
Rounding decimals	Newspaper Math.........................52	
Determining ratios	Food for Thought......................48	
Measurement and scale	On Vacation.................................50 Design a Zoo 54	
Geometric measurement	Design a Zoo ....54 3-D Shapes.................................56 Mathematical Windows 58	
Pythagorean theorem	Design a Zoo ....54 Mathematical Windows 58	
Basic geometry and spatial reasoning	Design a Zoo ....54 3-D Shapes.................................56 Mathematical Windows 58	
Identifying patterns and relationships	Show Me the Money ....46 Food for Thought......................48 The Missing Link ....60 Mock Math Election 66	

Matrix of Skills (continued)

Skill/State Standard	Activity	Page
Deciphering word problems	Backward Word Problems	64
Applying problem-solving and reasoning strategies	Newspaper Math	52
	The Missing Link	60
	Average Joe	62
	Backward Word Problems	64
	What's Your Problem?	70
Statistics, data analysis, and probability	Newspaper Math	52
	Average Joe	62
	Mock Math Election	66
	Wall Street	68
Identifying mean, median, mode, and range	On Vacation	50
	Average Joe	62
Interpreting data in alternative forms	Newspaper Math	52
	Wall Street	68
Representing data in alternative forms	Show Me the Money	46
	Food for Thought	48
	On Vacation	50
	Newspaper Math	52
	3-D Shapes	56
	Mock Math Election	66
	Wall Street	68
Estimating and making projections	Show Me the Money	46
	On Vacation	50
	Wall Street	68

Show Me the Money

Description

In this activity, students will simulate the experience of taking out a loan to purchase a big-ticket item such as a bicycle, stereo, or car. They will determine the best interest rates they can get based on their credit ratings, calculate payment amounts they can afford, and project the total amounts they will pay over time in principal and in interest. Finally, they will create graphs to illustrate their results.

<table>
<tr><td>

Skills/State Standards

✗ Algebraic equations, formulas, and applications

✗ Estimating and making projections

✗ Identifying patterns and relationships

✗ Calculating percentages, fractions, and decimals

✗ Representing data in alternative forms

</td></tr>
</table>

Materials You Need

- *Show Me the Money* reproducible (page 72)
- Details on interest rates and loan terms for students
- Sample item and loan information
- Index cards
- Overhead projector and supplies

Getting Ready

Use the Internet or local loan agencies to determine the current interest rates and terms for small loans. Have this information available for students to use. If time allows, students could do their own on-line research to find the best interest rates available.

Develop a credit rating and financial background scenario for each group of students. Write each scenario on a separate index card. Students will use these assigned credit ratings to complete the activity.

Make student handouts using the *Show Me the Money* reproducible.

Introducing the Activity

Ask students to think of items they would like to purchase if they had the money. Tell them that when most people buy homes or cars, they take out loans that are paid back in monthly installments. Explain that the key to making a loan a positive endeavor is to make sure that the terms of the loan work well with a person's budget and financial situation. If a person becomes financially overextended, he runs the risk of ruining his credit rating and even losing the item he was trying to purchase.

Review how a loan works, how a person qualifies for a loan, and what a credit rating is. Explain to students that at their age, they probably have not built up credit histories yet, but in this activity, they will see what it is like to take out a loan for a big-ticket item. Tell students that they will seek out the best loan terms and interest rates based on their credit ratings, and then show their results in a series of graphs. Remind them that they are developing skills they will use both now (on the standardized tests) and in the future (when they become adults).

Modeling the Activity

1. If you choose to divide the activity into sections, model the activity in steps so students can mirror your example.
2. Using an overhead transparency, share with students the item you have decided to purchase. Write down the relevant details of the item: make and model, cost, etc.
3. Discuss your simulated personal financial details: your credit rating, budget, financial commitments, etc.
4. Show students the different loans you could qualify for based on your credit rating. Calculate different loan scenarios based on varying terms (interest rates and payment amounts). Discuss whether you need to rethink the amount you can borrow or the item you have selected in order to find a better match between your budget and a loan.
5. Display your findings in a series of graphs, comparing the loan rates and payments over time. Discuss how the interest rate and payment schedule of a loan can make a big difference in the total amount you actually pay by the conclusion of the loan.

Activity in Practice

1. Divide the class into pairs or small teams. Distribute copies of the *Show Me the Money* handout and have each team select an item to purchase.
2. Give each team a card that shows a credit rating and financial situation to use for the activity. Then, distribute loan term information or allow students to research the best loans based on their credit ratings.
3. As students work to determine what loan is best for the team, remind them that they will need to show their findings in a series of graphical representations, such as three separate graphs for three different interest rates and payment amounts.
4. Have students display their completed graphs and share which types of loans they chose and why. Discuss with them how they can apply these skills to solve problems on the test they will take, as well as use this experience to make smart money choices in the future.

Extension

This activity could be broadened to include budgets and other financial purchases which students could chart over time, such as learning how a credit card works or maintaining a savings account.

Food for Thought

Description

In this activity, students will use data from their own eating habits to calculate percentages and fractions, determine ratios, and make projections. By keeping food journals, students will record and analyze the nutritional value of what they eat, then measure their daily intakes. They will compare these results to recommended daily allowances. Based on their findings, they will determine what changes should be made in their diets, chart these results, and make projections about their health.

***

Skills/State Standards

✗ Calculating percentages, fractions, and decimals

✗ Determining ratios

✗ Representing data in alternative forms

✗ Identifying patterns and relationships

***

Materials You Need

- *Food Journal* reproducible (page 73)
- *Food for Thought* reproducible (page 74)
- Recommended daily nutritional allowances and daily caloric intake ranges for students
- "Nutrition Facts" labels from several different foods
- Materials for making graphs or charts (poster board, markers, graph paper, etc.)
- Overhead projector and supplies

Getting Ready

Make student handouts using the *Food Journal* and *Food for Thought* reproducibles. Have each student keep a food journal for a designated period of time after you introduce the activity, but before students practice it. Create a sample journal entry on a transparency to use for modeling.

Make several transparencies that show "Nutrition Facts" labels from food packaging, as well as nutritional information for a few fruits and vegetables that do not come in packages. Then, print out and make a transparency of the USDA's Food Guide Pyramid and Daily Values. You should be able to find this information at *www.nutrition.gov*.

Introducing the Activity

Ask students if they know the saying, "You are what you eat." Then, ask if they know what is in their favorite foods— both the good and the bad. Tell students that in this activity, they will analyze what they eat to see how they measure up as healthy eaters. Explain that they will keep food journals to record and evaluate the nutritional values in their diets. They will then use that data to make comparisons, exercise their percentage and fraction skills, determine ratios, and make graphs.

Modeling the Activity

1. Show students the transparency you made of the nutrition facts information from several different foods. Explain that the percentages listed are always based on one serving. Remind students that they can look at the packaging or a USDA reference chart to find nutritional information on particular foods. As you look over the examples, be sure to discuss the following points:

   - Serving size per package/container
   - Percentage or fraction of the package/container represented by one serving
   - Calories per serving and per package/amount
   - Percentage/fractional breakdown of major components: fat, cholesterol, sodium, carbohydrates, protein, vitamins, and minerals
   - How the food item compares to the USDA's recommended Daily Values

2. Point out that the USDA's Daily Values are based on a certain number of calories consumed per day by an individual—on most packages, this is 2,000 calories. Clarify that the caloric needs of a person are determined by several factors, including age, gender, and lifestyle. For example, active teenage boys require about 2,800 calories per day, while active teenage girls require about 2,200 calories per day.

3. Using an overhead projector, show students your sample food journal entry. Select one meal from that day and determine the amount and type of calories consumed, the nutritional breakdown of the meal (fat, cholesterol, sodium, carbohydrate, and protein), and percentages of vitamins and minerals consumed.

4. Use those results to show students how to determine percentages and fractional amounts of the food items. From that information, make a chart or graph comparing the recommended daily percentages or fractions to your example day's total.

5. Explain that in their teams, students will do the same calculations and compare their results, determining which team members are the healthiest based on what they eat.

Activity in Practice

1. Divide the class into teams of three students. Before the activity begins, have students use the *Food Journal* handout to track their eating habits for one day, week, or month. Tell students that the better journals they keep, the more accurate their results will be.

2. Distribute copies of the *Food for Thought* handout. Have students use their food journals to complete the handout and then make graphs or charts representing the data.

3. Once they are finished, have each team determine which member is the healthiest. After teams present their results to the class, discuss with students how they applied mathematical skills to something they do every day—eat.

Extension

Students could compare the qualities of different foods, examining taste versus nutritional value. Based on their findings, they could propose a healthy snack list for the other students.

On Vacation

Description

In this activity, each student team will work together to plan a vacation. In planning their trip, students will first determine a budget by estimating costs, then represent this information graphically in a pie chart. They will map out their travel route by measuring the distances and representing them in a scale. They will also calculate how long it will take to reach each destination along their route. Next, they will research actual costs for specific categories. They will calculate the mean, median, mode, and range for each, and compare this information graphically with their estimations. Finally, they will present their information as a "pitch" to budget-conscious travelers.

Skills/State Standards

✗ Numbers and their operations

✗ Calculating percentages, fractions, and decimals

✗ Estimating and making projections

✗ Identifying mean, median, mode, and range

✗ Measurement and scale

✗ Representing data in alternative forms

Materials You Need

- *On Vacation* reproducibles (pages 75–77)
- Vacation plans, budget, costs, and graphs for modeling the activity
- Internet access, travel books, and atlases for student reference
- Overhead projector and supplies

Getting Ready

In order to model the activity for students, prepare a mini vacation plan of your own. Begin by creating a simple map, with a scale, that shows your travel route. Include the travel times and distances involved. Next, break down your overall vacation budget into specific categories (travel costs, accommodations, meals, entertainment, tips/gratuities, purchases, etc.) and estimate a dollar amount for each. Represent this budget in the form of a pie chart, calculating a percentage for each dollar amount. Then, research the actual costs for all aspects of your budget. Find three possibilities for each category. Select one option from each category as your final choice and create a revised pie chart based on the prices you found in your research. Prepare transparencies to help you share your information and graphs as discussed under "Modeling the Activity" on page 51.

This activity may require additional research time. Schedule some time when students can use the library or computer lab to do research on travel costs.

Make student handouts using the *On Vacation* reproducibles.

Introducing the Activity

Ask students what their ideal vacations would be like. Would they travel to many different locations or choose just one or two places to explore? Discuss what preparations they would have to make in order to make it a smooth trip. Tell students that in this activity they will work with partners to plan all aspects of a vacation, using key math skills along the way.

Modeling the Activity

1. Discuss the different aspects of a travel budget, including travel costs, accommodations, meals, entertainment, tips/gratuities, and purchases.
2. Share the itinerary you planned for a mini vacation. Explain how you plan to reach your destination, showing students the simple map you created. Demonstrate how you determined the total travel time and distance involved. Discuss the cost of tickets, the amount of gas needed, or the cost of a rental car based on your plans.
3. Discuss how the planning of a vacation involves doing research to make sure you get the best deals. Show students your price comparisons for travel, hotels, and other major expenditure categories. Then, show students how to determine the mean, median, mode, and range for each category you researched, using at least three prices per category.
4. Show students a comparison between your initial budget and actual costs. Then, represent your comparison in the form of a histogram, double bar graph, or line graph.
5. If time allows, estimate how much money you would spend each day over the course of the trip. Develop a graph to display your expenditures.

Activity in Practice

1. Divide the class into pairs or small teams. Pass out copies of the *On Vacation* handouts. Set a budget for each team to work with, or have students determine their own budgets.
2. Ask students to work through the handouts. In Part 1, they will break down their budgets and estimate costs for each category.
3. As they plan and map out their itineraries in Parts 2 and 3, students may need to use the Internet or atlases for reference. Provide library or computer lab research time, if needed.
4. Suggest that each team member work on a separate aspect of the budget for Part 4. Students can then share their findings in order to complete Part 5.
5. Once all of the teams are finished, have them present their information in the form of a sales pitch for traveling to their selected destinations. Presentations should highlight features from the students' research that would appeal to the budget-conscious traveler.

Extensions

Have students write travelogues about how planning their vacations forced them to use math in unexpected ways. The activity can also be broken down or shortened to focus on specific skills that students need to practice.

Newspaper Math

Description

In this activity, students will apply a variety of math skills to information found in newspaper articles. The skills they apply will vary with the article used. In some cases, they may take numbers and figures quoted in an article to make estimations, convert percents to fractions, round decimals, or represent data in alternative forms. In other cases, they may study a chart and use the data to describe and develop other relationships and ratios, or use the given statistics to conduct their own surveys and gather data. In still other cases, students may use relationships discussed in articles to develop word problems and then graph the results.

Skills/State Standards

- ✗ Rounding decimals
- ✗ Numbers and their operations
- ✗ Interpreting data in alternative forms
- ✗ Calculating percentages, fractions, and decimals
- ✗ Representing data in alternative forms
- ✗ Statistics, data analysis, and probability
- ✗ Applying problem-solving and reasoning strategies

Materials You Need

- *Newspaper Math* reproducible (page 78)
- Copies of recent newspapers
- Materials for making graphs or charts (poster board, markers, graph paper, etc.)
- Overhead projector and supplies

Getting Ready

Make student handouts using the *Newspaper Math* reproducible. Then, look through recent newspapers to find a variety of articles with some mathematical content. You will need articles to use as examples while you model the activity, as well as a small selection of articles for each team of students to use during the activity itself. Select two sample articles: one that includes a graph or chart and one that does not. Make a transparency of

each article or make copies for your students. Showing students articles with a range of different math applications will give them a nice, broad base of ideas to draw on during the activity.

Introducing the Activity

Read aloud the headline of a newspaper article that deals with numbers. Ask students to guess how numbers might be involved in the story: Does it discuss a survey or poll? Does it include statistics about a new trend? Does it involve economic or business information, or describe win and loss records for a local sports team? Explain to students that they can see how math is applied in the real world just by looking at a newspaper.

Tell students that in this activity they will use newspaper articles to apply different mathematical operations and skills. They will work in teams to select articles with mathematical possibilities to study relationships, create and graph data, develop word problems and equations, and use quantitative reasoning to solve problems and draw conclusions.

Modeling the Activity

1. Pass out copies of your sample article with a graph or chart, or place your transparency of the article on the overhead projector. Read the article together as a class and discuss how the graph relates to the content of the article. Talk about how students can draw conclusions about the relationships described in the article by looking at the content in connection with how the corresponding data is displayed.

2. With the students' input, develop a word problem, expression, or equation based on the information in the article and graph. Explain how the content of the article determined the type of mathematical approach you took.

3. Next, show students a sample article without a chart or graph. Work with the students to pull out numerical data from the article and use it to develop a table or graph. Depending on the article, you may decide to develop an equation first and then graph the results of the equation. This will show students the progression of mathematical applications.

4. Review the different types of expressions, equations, and graphical displays students can use during the practice portion of the activity. Also, discuss which sections of the newspaper may be rich in articles containing numerical and mathematical potential.

Activity in Practice

1. Divide the class into small teams. Distribute copies of the *Newspaper Math* handout and give each team a set of articles.

2. Have students divide their articles into the categories described on the handout. Then, have them select one or more of each kind to complete each section of the activity. As students work together in their teams, circulate around the room and offer suggestions as needed.

3. Once the teams have completed the steps on the handout, have them enlarge their graphical representations to display in the classroom. If any teams selected the same articles, compare their results as a class, discussing the approaches and methods each team used to complete the activity.

Extensions

As a variation, give students newspaper articles with all existing graphical representations of data removed. Then, have the students work in teams to develop their own tables, graphs, or charts. Have the students compare their own graphs to the originals included in the articles.

Simplify this activity by having students first look for articles, then develop short written proposals describing what they might do mathematically with the information presented in the articles. Using those proposals, work as a class to collect and calculate data, create graphs or equations, and draw conclusions. For further practice, students could work in small teams on one article using a teacher-suggested process.

Design a Zoo

Description

In this activity, students will work in small teams to design a zoo. They will plan the space needed, determine the necessary materials and projected costs, and create a scale map of the zoo. As they complete the activity, students will practice basic measurement and geometry skills, including finding perimeter, area, and volume. They will also estimate and compare costs for building the spaces, as well as the annual costs for maintaining the animals.

Skills/State Standards

X Measurement and scale

X Basic geometry and spatial reasoning

X Geometric measurement

X Pythagorean theorem

X Algebraic equations, formulas, and applications

X Mathematical and algebraic reasoning

Materials You Need

- *Design a Zoo* reproducibles (pages 79–82)
- Examples of zoo or park maps
- Information about one animal and its living space for modeling the activity
- Basic drawing supplies (colored markers, pencils, art paper, etc.)
- Overhead projector and supplies

Getting Ready

Make student handouts using the *Design a Zoo* reproducibles. Then, gather scale maps of parks, zoos, and other public spaces to share with students. Select an animal and its living space from one of the zoo plans. Calculate the costs of creating the space based on some research about the animal and its needs. Create overhead transparencies to show students the design of the space.

This activity may require additional research time. Schedule some time when students can use the library or computer lab to do research on their selected animals.

Introducing the Activity

Ask students to share memories about a trip to the zoo: What animals did they see? How were the animals' habitats designed? How was the zoo arranged? Next, ask students to think about the purpose of a zoo and why its design is so important. Explain that many mathematical details go into the design and construction of a zoo. Tell students that in this activity they will plan and design their own zoos. Using measurement, scale, basic geometry, estimation, and other mathematical operations, they will plan spaces, create scale drawings, and estimate costs.

Modeling the Activity

1. Use an overhead projector or LCD multimedia projector to show students a plan of the zoo you selected as an example. Show them how the living space of your chosen animal fits into the overall plan of the zoo.

2. Explain how the design of the animal's living space corresponds to its needs and reflects its natural habitat. For example, if the selected animal is a polar bear, the space is probably fairly large, has a swimming area, and so on.

3. Show students how to calculate the perimeter, area, and volume of the animal's space, and explain how these measurements relate to the materials needed to construct the space. Talk about the different types of materials used to create different spaces. Then, based on your selected animal, show students how to calculate the amount of materials that are needed to create the animal's space, using the geometric measurements discussed above. Remind students that they will be designing living areas for animals based on the animals' needs and drawing plans to scale for each space.

4. Based on research about the animal's diet and other needs, estimate the weekly, monthly, and annual costs of food and care for the animal. Construct a table and create some form of graphical display for these costs. Explain that students will work in teams to research the costs of caring for their animals and create graphs to help them compare these costs.

Activity in Practice

1. Divide the class into teams and distribute copies of the *Design a Zoo* handouts. Assign specific animals to each team, or let students decide what animals to include in their zoos. You can also give each team a range for the total size of their zoo and have them work within that range.

2. Have students work through each section of the handouts. Each team member will be responsible for one or more animals and should complete the handouts based on those animals. Then, the team can discuss how the animal spaces fit together into the overall layout of the zoo.

3. Once the teams have completed their handouts, have them present their zoo plans to the class. Consider displaying their maps and graphs in a public space in the school—the library, cafeteria, or hallways—so that other students can see their projects.

4. Upon completion of the activity, discuss with students the different mathematical skills they applied as they designed the zoos. Remind them that they can use what they learned to help them solve word problems involving measurement, estimation, and geometry on the standardized tests they will take.

Extension

This activity could be broken down to isolate and emphasize particular skills as they are learned in the course of the curriculum. As students are introduced to each mathematical concept that is used in the activity, they could apply that concept or skill by completing another phase of the zoo project.

3-D Shapes

Description

In this activity, students will work in teams to make a series of three-dimensional figures by stacking cubes. They will then make three-dimensional drawings of the figures they created. Teams will exchange drawings and try to determine how many cubes were used to create each figure. They will represent these numbers in the form of a top-view, nine-square grid drawing. As an extension, students may also calculate the volume of each figure.

Skills/State Standards

X Basic geometry and spatial reasoning
X Representing data in alternative forms
X Geometric measurement

Figure A

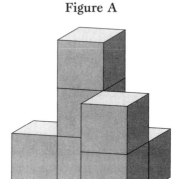

Materials You Need

- *3-D Shapes* reproducible (page 83)
- Plastic or wooden cubes for students to use to create three-dimensional figures (27 per team)
- Index cards
- Overhead projector and supplies

Getting Ready

Create your own three-dimensional figure using one set of cubes. Design your figure on a nine-cube base. (You do not have to use all 27 cubes in your design.) Once you have constructed your figure, create a three-dimensional drawing of it on the top half of a transparency sheet. (See Figure A.) On the lower half of the transparency, create a two-dimensional drawing of the same figure, using a nine-square grid. Write the number of cubes stacked in each position on the grid. (See Figure B.) Use these drawings during the modeling segment of the activity.

Make student handouts using the *3-D Shapes* reproducible.

Figure B

1	3	1
0	0	2
0	0	0

Introducing the Activity

Ask students if they have ever played tic-tac-toe, checkers, or chess. Ask them to describe what those game boards look like. Next, have the students imagine that the checkerboard patterns of the boards are constructed with a single layer of cubes rather than flat squares. Then, have them imagine that each cube is actually a stack of cubes, and that each stack varies in height.

Explain that the difference between a flat playing board and one stacked with cubes is the difference between a two-dimensional and three-dimensional view. Tell students that visualizing the difference between two and three dimensions is a skill they will need when applying spatial reasoning and when representing geometric shapes as solid forms.

Tell students that in this activity, they will practice visualizing the difference between two and three dimensions by drawing figures in both formats.

Modeling the Activity

1. Using the overhead projector, show students the three-dimensional drawing of the figure you created in the "Getting Ready" section.
2. Ask students to tell you how many cubes you used to create your figure. Take a set of cubes and reconstruct the figure to verify the total number of cubes used. Then, ask students how you could represent the total number of cubes in a two-dimensional drawing.
3. After discussing the possibilities, show students your completed nine-square grid, or two-dimensional drawing. Explain how the number written in each square represents the number of cubes stacked in that position of your three-dimensional figure.

Activity in Practice

1. Divide the class into small teams. Give each team a set of 27 cubes, several index cards, and a copy of the *3-D Shapes* handout. Setting a time limit, have students work to create a series of three-dimensional figures, each designed on a nine-cube base. Ask the teams to draw each of their creations three-dimensionally on a separate index card.
2. Once they have all finished, have each team exchange cards with another team and complete Part 2 of the handout.
3. After all teams have completed both parts of the handout, have each team select the most challenging or interesting drawing from the cards they received. As a class, come up with two-dimensional drawings for the selected figures.

Extensions

As an alternative, have students work in teams to construct three-dimensional figures with cubes, then draw a top view of each figure on a nine-square grid. Have each team exchange drawings with another team and try to draw that team's figures three-dimensionally.

In another version of this activity, students could create three-dimensional structures or buildings using a variety of geometric solids. Teams could then rotate around the classroom, calculating the surface area and volume of the other teams' structures.

Mathematical Windows

Description

In this activity, students will use their knowledge of geometry to design stained glass windows. Working in small teams, students will create unique designs that incorporate a predetermined number and assortment of basic plane figures. Once their designs are complete, students will use them to perform a variety of mathematical calculations. They will measure angles and apply the Pythagorean theorem, as well as determine perimeter, area, circumference, and diameter.

> ### Skills/State Standards
> X Basic geometry and spatial reasoning
> X Geometric measurement
> X Pythagorean theorem

Materials You Need

- *Mathematical Windows* reproducible (page 84)
- Examples of stained glass window patterns
- Art supplies and materials for making stained glass windows (construction paper, brightly colored tissue paper, scissors, tape, glue, etc.)
- Overhead projector and supplies

Getting Ready

Find examples of stained glass window patterns in books and magazines to share with students. Use these images to illustrate how different shapes can fit together to create cohesive designs.

Choose one stained glass window design to use when you model the activity. Make a color copy of the design on a transparency. On a separate transparency, calculate the perimeter and area of a few of the shapes included in the design.

Make student handouts using the *Mathematical Windows* reproducible.

Introducing the Activity

Ask students to look around the room to find examples of various geometric shapes: circles, squares, triangles, trapezoids, parallelograms, etc. Explain that the designs of many common-place items, such as furniture, cars, and buildings, are based on geometric shapes.

Explain to students that they are about to become window designers. In this activity, they will create unique stained glass windows that incorporate a variety of geometric shapes into their designs. Students will then use their understanding of geometry to determine degrees of angles, apply the Pythagorean theorem, and calculate a range of geometric measurements.

Modeling the Activity

1. Display the transparency you made of a stained glass window design. Ask students to point out the simple plane figures included in the design. Discuss how the different shapes fit together to form a cohesive pattern and overall design.
2. Select one of the shapes in the window and determine its perimeter and area. Explain to students that when they design their own windows, they will have to use each window's perimeter to help them determine the measurements of every shape within the design.
3. Tell students that they will be required to include a number of specific geometric shapes and angles in their designs. However, they will have the freedom to arrange these required elements in any way they like and to add other shapes to the design as well.

Activity in Practice

1. Divide the class into small teams.
2. Give each team a copy of the *Mathematical Windows* handout. Decide upon the window size, minimum number of shapes, and specific types of shapes and angles that must be included in every team's design. Have students make these notes in Part 1 of the handout.
3. Display examples of stained glass window patterns around the classroom. As students work with their teams on their own designs, encourage them to look at these patterns for inspiration and ideas.
4. Once teams have sketched out their designs, have them create large-scale, colorful versions of the windows to display in the classroom. Provide black construction paper for students to use when making the frames for their windows. Using brightly colored tissue paper for the geometric shapes will create a stained-glass effect and allow light to filter through.
5. Ask teams to calculate and record the measurements of each shape in their designs.

Extensions

As an alternative to this activity, have students look at places in and around the school to find examples of geometric shapes, both two- and three-dimensional. Lines on sports fields, food in the cafeteria, objects in the classroom, and even school buildings lend themselves easily to working with geometric measurements.

Have students study reproductions of famous works of art and break them down into basic geometric shapes. If possible, have students measure the various shapes and angles.

For practice determining the surface area and volume of geometric solids, have students consider the shapes in their windows as three-dimensional. They could even construct three-dimensional models of their windows using common objects.

5

The Missing Link

Description

In this activity, students will practice identifying patterns and relationships. They will also use quantitative reasoning to determine the missing information, steps, or sections in a problem or pattern. As a class, students will be given a series of cards containing parts of a pattern or steps to a problem, with pieces of each purposely omitted. Students must then share their pieces of the mathematical puzzles with each other and try to fit them together in order to complete the patterns or solve the problems.

Skills/State Standards

X Identifying patterns and relationships

X Applying problem-solving and reasoning strategies

Materials You Need

- *The Missing Link* reproducible (page 85)
- Index cards (plain and colored)
- Overhead projector and supplies

Getting Ready

To prepare for the modeling portion of the activity, copy one word problem, one pattern, and one multi-step problem onto a transparency, omitting one or more crucial pieces of information from each. Here is a sample word problem and pattern you could use:

> Every weekend, Mr. Hendricks drives 50 miles from his house in the city to his cabin. His average speed during the trip is 45 mph. How long does it take for him to get there?
>
> HEAD to TAIL: head, heal, teal, tell, tall, tail

Prepare several other problems and patterns to use for the activity. Write down the different steps to the problems and pieces of the patterns on index cards, with each step or piece on a separate card. In order to ease students into the activity, you may wish to color-code the problem or pattern cards, or create puzzle-like pieces that fit together. As the students get more practice with this activity, make the shapes and colors of the cards uniform, forcing students to do more sleuthing in order to identify the patterns and figure out the problems.

Make student handouts using *The Missing Link* reproducible.

Introducing the Activity

Ask students to complete this pattern: A, __, C. Explain that the alphabet is an example of a pattern or sequence, just like a series of numbers. Next, ask students how they would solve this problem: If A = 1 and B = 2, what is A + B? Explain that patterns and problems include necessary parts that can each be used as a clue in identifying the pattern or solving the problem.

Remind students that knowing how to recognize patterns and steps is a skill they will need both in everyday life and on the standardized tests they will take. Tell students that in this activity, they will use their sleuthing skills to detect the missing links in problems and patterns. They will work in small teams to figure out what elements are missing in order to solve each problem or isolate each pattern.

Modeling the Activity

1. Using the transparency you prepared, present a word problem to students and ask them to try to solve it. As they apply the problem-solving process, guide them to identify what information is missing and what they need to know in order to find the solution.

2. Next, present a pattern to students with one part missing. Have them work together as a class to identify the pattern and the missing element.

3. Finally, present a problem that involves several steps, but exclude one of the steps in the process. Have students work as a class to identify the missing step. Explain to students that they can use the backwards strategy to help them solve this type of problem. That is, they can work the problem in reverse, beginning with the solution and working backward until they find the missing step.

4. Tell students that in this activity, they will have to work together and apply problem-solving skills in order to figure out the missing links in different patterns and problems.

Activity in Practice

1. Distribute cards containing problem steps or pattern parts, giving each student one card. The number of patterns or problems circulating on the cards will depend on the number of students and steps or parts involved.

2. Instruct students to circulate around the room, sharing the information on their cards in order to find other classmates with parts or steps to the same pattern or problem.

3. Once students have formed their teams, give each team a copy of the *Missing Link* handout. Ask the students to work together to complete the handout. They will be asked to describe the information they have been given on the cards, identify and record the missing link, explain their reasoning process in writing, and determine the solution or identify the pattern.

4. After all of the teams have completed their handouts, ask them to share their experiences with the rest of the class. Have students discuss the ways they solved the math mysteries and how these skills are transferable to what they may see on a standardized test.

Extension

For more advanced practice, have students develop their own missing links problems and patterns. Encourage students to use their textbooks or other materials in order to generate ideas. Then, have them work in small teams to develop different types of word problems and patterns, cleverly removing one detail, step, or element from each. When they are finished, have students trade their creations with other teams who must figure out what is missing and solve the problems or isolate the patterns.

Average Joe

Description

In this activity, students will work in small teams to analyze a series of test scores. Together with their teams, they will determine which statistical measurement (mean, median, mode, or range) presents the most accurate picture of each set of scores. Students will then discuss the different statistics and explain what factors contributed to their decisions. Finally, they will be asked to add or change test scores in order to alter the outcome.

Skills/State Standards

✗ Identifying mean, median, mode, and range

✗ Statistics, data analysis, and probability

✗ Applying problem-solving and reasoning strategies

Materials You Need

• Index cards
• Overhead projector and supplies

Getting Ready

To prepare for this activity, you will need to create one set of test or quiz scores for each team of students. Use made-up scores or grades from a different or previous year's class. Include between 18 and 30 scores in each set. Write each set of scores on a separate index card.

You may also choose to prepare one sample set of scores (or other numbers, such as age or height) to use when modeling the activity. Write out these numbers on a transparency to use with the overhead projector. Determine the mean, median, mode, and range of the numbers ahead of time. It may be helpful to tweak the set a bit so that the mode or median presents a more accurate picture of the set than the mean does.

Introducing the Activity

Review the different types of statistics that are familiar to your students: mean, median, mode, and range. Ask students to describe what each term means. Which statistic do they see or use the most often? Explain that while the average, or mean, may be the statistic that seems to be used the most—especially in calculating grades—it is not always the best measure of a specific group of numbers. Ask students to consider the following example:

A successful software company has just five employees. The CEO of the company makes $250,000 a year, while each of the other four employees has an annual salary of just $30,000.

Based on the information in the example, the mean salary for the company is $74,000—considerably higher than the salary of every employee except for the CEO. The mode and median of the salaries are both $30,000. This seems to give a more accurate picture of the typical employee's salary than the mean does.

Point out to students how the range can sometimes give an indication of which statistic may be best to use. In the case of the example, the range is $220,000—a pretty significant number. A narrow range usually indicates that the mean will provide a reasonable picture of the numbers. A broad range indicates that another statistic may be more appropriate to use.

Modeling the Activity

Show students the sample set of scores or other numbers you prepared. Review the formulas for calculating mean, median, mode, and range. Use your sample set of scores to calculate all four statistics. Ask students to tell you which statistic gives the most accurate picture of the numbers.

Activity in Practice

1. Divide the class into small teams.
2. Give each team an index card that lists a set of test scores to use in the activity.
3. Have students calculate the mean, median, mode, and range for their given scores.
4. Ask each team to write a few sentences discussing which measure they think most accurately describes how the students performed on the test.
5. Next, ask students to alter the test scores to change the outcomes. Discuss the results.
6. If desired, ask each team to make a small presentation to the class about their findings.

Extension

Students can use their own test, quiz, or homework scores to calculate statistics. Have students work individually to determine how high or low they must score on future tests in order to maintain or raise their averages.

Backward Word Problems

Description

If your students have difficulty translating words on a page into solvable equations, try this activity. In this exercise, students will create word problems based on equations or expressions from their math textbook. They will then collaborate to solve the problems. Finally, students will record the problem-solving steps they used. By using this backward approach, students will begin to see how numerical relationships described in words are essentially mathematical equations or expressions in disguise.

Skills/State Standards

✗ Deciphering word problems

✗ Mathematical and algebraic reasoning

✗ Algebraic equations, formulas, and applications

✗ Numbers and their operations

✗ Applying problem-solving and reasoning strategies

Materials You Need

- *Backward Word Problems* reproducible (page 86)
- Math textbooks
- Overhead projector and supplies

Getting Ready

Look through your students' math textbook to find equations and expressions to use with this activity. Assemble and photocopy a list of equations to make a handout for each team. Make student handouts using the *Backward Word Problems* reproducible.

Introducing the Activity

Ask students to solve the following equation for x: $3x = 15$.

After students say $x = 5$, ask them to solve this word problem:

> Brian used his birthday money to buy three CDs at the CD Exchange. The CDs were on discount and cost a total of $15. If all three CDs were priced the same, what was the cost of one CD?

Lead students to see that the equation $3x = 15$ represents the same relationship outlined in the above word problem. Discuss how word problems are basically mathematical expressions and equations just waiting to be discovered. Explain to students that their job as math experts is to figure out what the hidden expressions or equations are in order to solve the problems.

Tell students that one way to strengthen their skills in deciphering word problems is to work backwards, like they did with the sample equation. In this activity, students will see how the words and ideas in word problems actually represent variables and numbers. As a result, students will be more prepared to apply the same process in reverse when they encounter word problems on standardized tests.

Modeling the Activity

1. Using your students' math textbook as a source, select one equation or expression and write it on a transparency. Work with students to solve the problem and record the answer.
2. Next, ask students for suggestions about what some of the variables in the problem could represent. After discussing a few possibilities, develop a word problem based on the variables, the given numbers, and your solution to the equation or expression.
3. If students need additional modeling, select a more challenging equation or one that involves more than one operation in order to solve it. Use this equation to develop another word problem with additional information that may or may not be needed.
4. Discuss how some word problems include extraneous information or require more than one operation or process to solve. Tell students that they may want to use graphs or charts to track the relevant information in the problems during the activity.

Brian used his birthday money to buy three CDs at the CD Exchange. The CDs were on discount and cost a total of $15. If all three CDs were priced the same, what was the cost of one CD?

Activity in Practice

1. Divide the class into small teams and distribute copies of the *Backward Word Problems* handout. Provide each team with a list of possible equations or expressions to use for the activity, or ask students to select one or more equation or expression from the math textbook themselves.
2. Have students follow the steps on the handout to solve their selected equations and to develop related word problems.
3. Once the teams have finished, ask them to share their equations and word problems with the class. Another possibility is to have the teams share just their word problems. The rest of the class can then try to figure out what equation or expression was used as the basis for each problem.

Extension

As an alternative activity, students could work in teams to create skits that involve some type of relationship, change, or problem. The rest of the class could work together to determine what the relationship, change, or problem is, then convey it in mathematical terms and solve it.

Mock Math Election

Description

In this activity, students will simulate an election environment in order to collect information and analyze data. They will develop surveys based on actual school issues or on the platforms of real or "math-made" candidates, and then use those surveys to poll the student population. Taking the information gathered in the polls, students will apply mathematical reasoning, analyze statistics, and identify patterns in order to make predictions. Over the course of the activity, students will rely on a variety of mathematical tools and processes. They will convert numbers to fractions and percentages; they will gather statistics and develop ratios and inequalities; and they will represent and interpret those statistics graphically to make predictions and draw conclusions. Finally, if applicable, students will compare their statistics to actual election results.

Skills/State Standards

X Statistics, data analysis, and probability

X Identifying patterns and relationships

X Mathematical and algebraic reasoning

X Representing data in alternative forms

Materials You Need

- Sample polls and surveys
- Overhead projector and supplies

Getting Ready

Search newspapers, magazines, and the Internet for examples of polls and surveys to share with your students. Try to gather a wide variety in order to provide students with a large frame of reference. You may also want to visit the Gallup Poll Web site for sample polls and ideas on question development: *http://www.gallup.com.*

As students collect and tabulate their survey results, they may want to use a spreadsheet program to help organize their information. If possible, make this resource available to students.

Introducing the Activity

Ask students to explain why we hold elections and how people choose to vote for certain candidates. Review the role that polls and surveys hold in the election process. Explain how math plays an important part in campaigns and elections, from calculating the percentage of support for a particular candidate to tabulating the votes to determine a winner.

Tell students that in this activity, they will assume the roles of pollsters and statisticians. As such, they will try to gauge people's attitudes about the platforms of actual or imaginary candidates. Explain that they will develop, administer, and analyze surveys and polls, and then use their data to draw conclusions and make predictions about the impending election.

Modeling the Activity

1. Show students several examples of previously published polls and surveys. Review the basics of developing a poll or survey, including who will be surveyed, the purpose of the survey, and what will be done with the information gathered. Looking at some sample questions, discuss the format (open-ended or closed) and style of the questions used.
2. Use a previously published poll or develop your own short list of questions to ask your students. Tally the students' responses to each question on an overhead transparency.
3. After the survey is completed, show students how to tabulate the totals for each question. Calculate the resulting percentages (25% agreed with number 1), fractional amounts (1/2 disagreed with number 2), ratios (3 out of 10 students said . . .), and inequalities (less than 30% are in favor of) based on the total number of people surveyed.
4. Use the calculations to develop a chart or table and some kind of graph, such as a bar graph, pie chart, histogram, or line graph.
5. Explain that students can use the results of a poll to draw conclusions about public opinion on certain issues. Then, from those conclusions, they can make predictions as to how a specific population may vote on an issue or for a candidate.

Activity in Practice

1. Decide whether students will base their polls and surveys on the current platform issues of actual candidates, their own "math-made" candidates, or on current school or local issues.
2. Divide the class into several teams. Then, decide whether each team will focus on a unique issue or platform position, or if all teams will use the same questions but develop different types of statistics and graphs from the results.
3. Provide a variety of surveys and polls for reference as the teams develop their questions.
4. Once each team has developed a poll or survey, have them collect responses by questioning the desired population. Suggest that students develop a data collection sheet (in the form of a chart with boxes) to record responses for each question.
5. After the surveys and polls have been administered and the results tabulated, have students develop graphs of the data.
6. If applicable, have students analyze their results in comparison with the outcomes of actual elections. How do the outcomes compare to the students' predictions?

Extension

Students could base their polls and surveys on polls found in the newspaper, then compare their own results to those described in the related articles.

Wall Street

Description

In this activity, students will assume the role of investors, "purchasing" stocks and tracing the performance of their portfolios over time. They will calculate gains and losses, represent the data in graphical form, and even project earnings based on current market trends. Students will gain valuable experience working with decimals and fractions, converting them to dollar amounts, and determining ratios.

Skills/State Standards

X Statistics, data analysis, and probability

X Interpreting data in alternative forms

X Representing data in alternative forms

X Estimating and making projections

X Calculating percentages, fractions, and decimals

Materials You Need

- *Stock Watcher* reproducible (page 87)
- *Wall Street* reproducibles (pages 88 and 89)
- Examples of newspaper stock pages
- Overhead projector and supplies

Getting Ready

This activity can be done in a variety of time frames—one week, one month, or even longer. The depth and breadth of the project will determine the time frame you choose, especially if you want to give students time to conduct initial research on companies before investing their money.

Make student handouts using the *Stock Watcher* and *Wall Street* reproducibles.

Introducing the Activity

Ask students what they know about stocks and the stock market. Explain that stocks represent shares in specific companies. Ask students what stocks they would buy if they had $10,000. How would they know which companies were strong and which were on a downslide? Discuss why the stock market can be a good place to invest money and how it can affect the economy. Explain that working with the stock market involves lots of math and that knowing how to invest one's money wisely is the sign of a math-smart investor.

Tell students that in this activity, they will work as investment teams to select stocks, purchase shares, and trace their earnings or losses over a given period of time. Explain that they will learn how to read the newspaper's stock pages in order to calculate gains or losses and to chart their investments graphically. They will also use their percentage and fraction skills, determine ratios, graph data, and even make projections based on market trends to estimate future earnings.

BFO 5K @ **61.25** ▼ **1.35**... **BFP** 1K @ **32.15** ▲ **.05**...

Modeling the Activity

1. Distribute copies of the *Stock Watcher* handout. Then, make copies of one stock listed in the stock pages, or create a fictitious stock listing and use an overhead transparency to show students the headings for each column. Discuss the meaning of each heading.

2. Point out the stock's purchase price, or beginning and ending prices, and how the price might have fluctuated. The paper may list the results in decimals or in fractions. Show students how to convert both types of listings into dollar amounts.

3. Simulate what you would have made or lost that day if you owned 100 shares of stock. Calculate what you would have made if you had bought the stock that day at the low price and sold it at the high price. Explain how looking at the price-to-earnings ratio and change, as well as the stock's performance over the last 52 weeks is a good start; but in order to be a truly smart investor, a person needs to research a company before purchasing stock.

4. Using your example stock, demonstrate how to make a simple line graph showing how your shares fared for the day, indicating any profits or losses. You may also want to show students several sample line graphs from the newspaper or on-line investment resources.

Activity in Practice

1. Divide the class into teams and give each student a copy of the *Wall Street* handouts. (The handouts are designed for a one-week investment period. If you plan to extend the project beyond one week, make additional copies of the handout.)

2. Explain that each team will collaborate to build an investment portfolio containing one stock per team member. Teams will choose stocks together and then decide how to divide the total amount of investment money among the chosen stocks. Each team member will become the expert for a particular stock in the portfolio and record all of the necessary information about that stock as outlined in the chart in Part 2 of the handout.

3. Remind students that they will need to confer with their teams about how each stock is doing, deciding whether to buy or sell a stock based on its daily highs and lows. Explain that they will be tracking their stocks' vital signs for one week (or longer) and then graphing their investment choices individually and as a team.

4. If your local paper lists stock prices or changes in decimals, consider having students convert the amounts into fractions. If your paper lists stock prices or changes in mixed numbers or fractions of a dollar, consider having students keep a log of their conversions from fractions into dollar decimal amounts. Students can then show their work for cash credits that can be applied toward their total available investment amount.

5. If desired, set up the activity in the form of a competition, with each team trying to make the smartest investment choices based on research. The team that "earns" the most money beyond its initial investments could win "bonus bucks" to use in the classroom.

Extension

For more practice with probability, have students compare their investments in the stock market to investments in various fixed accounts, such as savings accounts, mutual funds, or CDs. They could use probability to determine which type of investment might bring higher rewards over time.

What's Your Problem?

Description

In this activity, students will identify a problem in their school or community and then apply problem-solving strategies to develop a solution. As they work through the problem-solving process, students will draw upon related mathematical concepts and skills, using them in a real-world context. In this format, students will solve problems that arise in different contexts, apply and adapt a variety of strategies to solve these problems, and monitor and reflect on the process of mathematical problem solving they use.

> ### Skills/State Standards
> ✗ Applying problem-solving and reasoning strategies
> ✗ Mathematical and algebraic reasoning

Materials You Need

- *What's Your Problem?* reproducible (page 90)
- Overhead projector and supplies

Getting Ready

Make student handouts using the *What's Your Problem?* reproducible. Then, generate a list of sample problems or issues relevant to your school or community to use during the modeling portion of the activity. Each problem must involve mathematical operations and reasoning in some way.

Introducing the Activity

Ask students to define the word *problem*. After students share their definitions, discuss how the word can be used to describe a variety of situations and issues. Ask students to brainstorm some problems in their own community (school or city). Maybe the school needs a recycling program, or perhaps the city needs more bicycle paths. Discuss how math can be used to help solve problems on different levels—not just the problems found in textbooks.

Tell students that they will work in teams to identify a local problem and develop a solution that involves mathematical reasoning and skills. They will use these skills to incorporate math in their steps to solve the problem.

Modeling the Activity

1. Choose an example of a problem or issue in your school or local community that somehow involves mathematical operations and reasoning. For example, if the school does not currently recycle, what issues are involved in starting a recycling program? What would the costs, profits, and space requirements be?

2. Show students a problem-solving process that can be adapted to address the problem. Review the major steps involved in solving a mathematical problem, adding any applicable details as needed:

   - Define and understand the problem.
   - Gather and process information.
   - Formulate a plan.
   - Implement the plan.
   - Evaluate the plan.
   - Share the solution.

3. Discuss how each step of this problem-solving process would be applied to the sample issue or problem.

4. Remind students that they may need to develop an equation to help them solve the problem. Explain that an equation is simply a mathematical tool used to help people solve real-life problems. Have students think of real situations around them that might involve an equation of some kind. For example, if their school club had a fund-raiser last year, how much money do they think they will make this year? If they predict that they will make twice as much money this year, how can that prediction be expressed as an equation?

5. Show students how to assign a variable to represent the answer to the problem. Explain why using an algebraic expression whenever possible rather than simple arithmetic is good practice. The more students use equations to solve simple problems, the easier it will be for them to use equations to solve complex problems that require other techniques or strategies.

Activity in Practice

1. Divide the class into teams and distribute copies of the *What's Your Problem?* handout. Have students on each team work together to select an issue or problem that involves math in some way. If appropriate, provide students with the list of ideas you generated during the "Getting Ready" portion of the activity.

2. Once they have identified a problem, have each team work through the problem-solving process as described on the handout. Explain that it may be helpful to divide up the responsibilities for each part of the process.

3. After they have completed Steps 1–3 as outlined on the handout, have teams implement their plans and record their results.

4. After all of the teams have implemented their plans, have them evaluate the results, including the math involved in reaching their solutions.

5. Ask teams to present their plans and solutions to the rest of the class and discuss how math played a part in the problem-solving process.

Extension

If students have difficulty coming up with an issue or problem, assign each team a specific topic with the mathematical possibilities outlined for them.

Show Me the Money

Part 1. Complete the information about the item you want to purchase.

Name or description of item: _____

Cost of item: _____

Make and model of item: _____

Your credit rating: _____

Based on your credit rating, what types of loans do you qualify for?

_____

_____

Part 2. Complete the following chart for three different types of loans. Use the back of this sheet or a separate sheet of paper to show your work.

Name of Lender and Type of Loan	Interest Rate	Monthly Payment	Length of Loan	Total Amount Paid
1.				
2.				
3.				

Use the lines below to write any equations you used to determine the answers for the chart.

_____

_____

_____

Part 3. Using a separate sheet of paper, display your results by creating a graph or chart for each of the three loans above.

Name: _____ Date: _____

Food Journal

Directions: Keep track of everything you eat and drink for one day. Record the nutritional information in the chart below.

Date: _____

Food or Beverage	Servings	Calories	Fat	Cholesterol	Sodium	Carbohydrate	Protein

Food for Thought

Part 1. Using your food journal, calculate your total intake in each category for one day. Write your totals in the chart below.

Calories	Fat	Cholesterol	Sodium	Carbohydrate	Protein

Part 2. Use the space below to create a graph showing the percentages and/or fractional amounts of your total consumption for each category above. Then, compare your graph to the USDA's Daily Values, and make a second graph or chart showing the differences and similarities.

Part 3. Use a separate sheet of paper to create a graph (pie chart, line graph, bar graph, or other) that compares each team member's daily intake in each category to the USDA's recommended Daily Values.

On Vacation

Part 1. Determine your total vacation budget, using the chart below to divide your budget into the major categories you will need for your trip. Then, take the information from the chart and create a pie chart that breaks down your estimated budget.

Your total vacation budget: $ _____

Category	Dollar Amount	Percentage

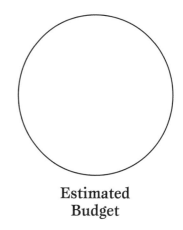

Estimated
Budget

Part 2. Plan your itinerary by determining where you will begin and end your trip, and how you will get around. Use the organizer below to map out your departure and return locations, along with two major stops along your trip. Calculate the distance between each point and the next, as well as how long it will take to make the trip.

Departure point: _____

Distance: _____   Travel time: _____

First stop: _____

Distance: _____   Travel time: _____

Second stop: _____

Distance: _____   Travel time: _____

Return to: _____

Major mode(s) of transportation: _____

Total distance: _____   Total travel time: _____

What formulas/equations did you use to determine the total distance and time of your trip?

_____

On Vacation (continued)

Part 3. Use the space below to map out your itinerary from your starting location to each destination and, finally, to your return location. Create a scale to represent the distance in miles between stops on your trip. Make sure to include the travel time for each leg of the trip.

Part 4. List your vacation budget categories in the first column of the chart. For each category, find at least three examples of prices and use those numbers to calculate the mean, median, mode, and range. Share your findings with your team and record your results in the chart.

Category	Mean Cost	Median Cost	Mode Cost	Range

On Vacation (continued)

Part 5. Compare the amounts from your estimated budget to the amounts you discovered when researching in Part 4. In the space below, make a new pie chart for your revised budget. Then, calculate the differences between your initial and revised budgets. Represent these differences in the form of a histogram, double bar graph, or line graph.

Newspaper Math

Directions: Divide your articles into the categories below. Follow the steps to apply mathematical processes to the information in each article. Show your work on another sheet of paper.

Articles WITH Tables, Graphs, or Charts

1. Study the relationship between the article and graphical display of data.

   • What is the article about? _____

   _____

   • What information is included in the table, graph, or chart? _____

   _____

   • What mathematical operations and processes
   are used or shown in the table, graph, or chart? _____

   _____

2. Develop a word problem, expression, or equation based on information from the article and the table, graph, or chart.

3. Draw and explain any conclusions from your results.

Articles WITHOUT Tables, Graphs, or Charts

1. Study the article for mathematical possibilities.

   • What is the article about? _____

   _____

   • What numbers or mathematical processes are involved in the article? _____

   _____

   • What types of tables, graphs, or charts could
   you create using information from the article? _____

   _____

2. Pull out any numerical information or data from the article.

3. Using the mathematical information in the article, develop a word problem, expression, or equation. Write down all of the steps and details involved.

4. Solve the problem or equation. Show your results in the form of a table, graph, or chart.

Design a Zoo

Part 1. Work with the members of your team to plan what types of animals you will care for at your zoo. Make a list of all of the animals. Then, determine which member of the team will research each animal. Use your findings to answer the questions that follow.

What animals will you have in your zoo?

_____

_____

Which animal will you research and design a living space for?

_____

What type of habitat will your animal need? _____

_____

What does the animal's diet consist of? _____

_____

What other requirements does the animal have? _____

_____

_____

Part 2. Plan a space for your animal. Based on your research, determine the size and type of space that your particular animal will require.

Minimum and maximum amount of space needed: _____

Shape of the planned space: _____

Area of the planned space: _____

Perimeter of the planned space: _____

Circumference/radius of the planned space (if applicable): _____

Volume of the planned space: _____

Design a Zoo (continued)

Part 3. Draw a two- or three-dimensional plan of your animal's living space below. First, decide on an appropriate scale for the drawing (for example, 1 inch = 10 feet). Then, use your measurements from Part 2 to create your plan.

Design a Zoo (continued)

Part 4. Based on your research, determine the cost of creating a living space for your animal. Complete the information in the chart below.

Materials Needed	Amount Needed	Average Cost of Material	Total Cost of Material

Part 5. Use the information from your chart to create a graph (bar graph, line graph, pie chart, histogram, or pictograph) comparing the costs of different materials needed to construct the space for your animal. Draw your graph in the space below.

Design a Zoo (continued)

Part 6. Based on your animal's diet and other needs, calculate the amount of food and other items needed per week, month, and year. Then, use your calculations to estimate the weekly, monthly, and annual costs of feeding and caring for the animal.

Foods/ Items Needed for Animal	Amount Needed per Week	Estimated Weekly Cost	Amount Needed per Month	Estimated Monthly Cost	Amount Needed per Year	Estimated Annual Cost

Part 7. Share the information from your charts in Parts 4 and 6 with the other members of your team. In the space below, create a graph that compares the costs of maintaining all of the animals in your zoo for a week, month, or year.

Part 8. Share your drawings and information with the other members of your team. Together, design a map, to scale, that includes all of the animals' living spaces. On your map, make sure to plan for other elements of the zoo as well, such as rest rooms, pedestrian pathways, storage areas, food and rest areas, and parking lots. Work as a team to draw the map. Include a scale to indicate the distance, size, or length of each element on your map.

3-D Shapes

Part 1. Use the space below or a separate sheet of paper to draw each three-dimensional figure your team creates. Copy each drawing onto an index card to trade with another team.

Part 2. Based on the three-dimensional drawings your team received, use the following nine-square grids to represent each figure two-dimensionally. Write the number of cubes in each stack in the appropriate box on the grid.

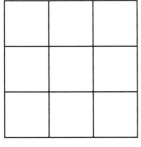 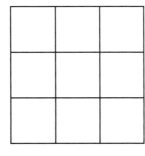 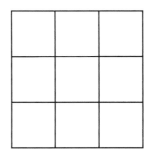

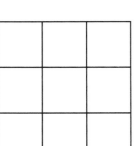 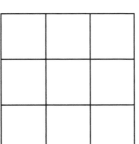 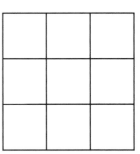

Mathematical Windows

Part 1. As you plan out your team's stained glass window design, begin by selecting the different geometric shapes you would like to include. Then, determine the overall shape and dimensions of your window and calculate its perimeter and area.

Your window must include at least _____ plane figures from the following list:

_____   _____   _____

_____   _____   _____

_____   _____   _____

What shape will your window be? _____

What will the perimeter of your window be? _____

What will the area of your window be? _____

Part 2. Draw a sketch of your stained glass window in the space below. Then, make a large-scale version of your design using construction paper and colorful tissue paper.

Part 3. Label each geometric shape in your sketch above with a different number. Then, on another sheet of paper, list all of the shapes in your design by number. Measure the large-scale version of your window to determine the perimeter (p), area (a), diameter (d), and circumference (c) of each shape as appropriate. List these measurements after each shape's number.

The Missing Link

Directions: Follow the steps to find the missing link in your problem or pattern.

Step 1. Look at the cards from every member of the team. Use the cards to record, in order, the steps of your problem or to sketch the pieces of your pattern in the space below.

Step 2. Looking back at the information recorded in Step 1, what is the missing link? Write or sketch your answer below.

Step 3. Explain the process you used to determine the missing link.

Step 4. Now that you have determined the missing link, use the space below to write out the solution or describe the pattern.

Backward Word Problems

Directions: Complete each of the following steps with your team. Be prepared to share your work.

Step 1. Choose an equation or expression as the basis for a word problem. Write it on the line below.

_____

Step 2. Solve the equation or expression and record your steps below. Use an additional sheet of paper if necessary.

_____

_____

_____

_____

Step 3. Develop a word problem based on your selected equation or expression. Write it in on the lines below.

_____

_____

_____

Step 4. How did your team come up with the idea for this word problem? Explain the steps you took to create the word problem based on the selected equation or expression.

_____

_____

_____

_____

Stock Watcher

This chart lists some of the common abbreviations and terms
you may see when looking at newspaper stock pages.

Sym (Symbol)	Abbreviation of a company's name used in stock listings
pf (preferred stock)	Owners of preferred stock are entitled to dividends before owners of common stock, and, if a business is sold, they are entitled to a share of the proceeds first
Vol (Volume)	Number of stock shares traded that day (multiply by 100 to find the actual number of shares)
hds (hundreds)	Measure of stock shares traded
Div (Dividend)	Amount of money paid quarterly by a company to its stockholders for each share of stock owned
Yld (Yield)	Dividend divided by price (usually given as a percentage)
P/E (Price-to-Earnings Ratio)	Relationship between stock price and earnings over the last four quarters (stock price divided by earnings per share)
High	Highest price for a stock that day
Low	Lowest price for a stock that day
Close	Price of a stock at the time the stock market closes for the day
Chg (Change)	Amount of increase or decrease in a stock's value that day

Wall Street

Your investment team has $_____ to invest.

Part 1. Use your money to invest in one stock per team member. You may divide the money among the stocks however you choose. In your team, decide what stocks you will purchase and how many shares of each. You may need to do some research on the companies before making your decisions.

Write the name of each stock and its symbol on the lines below.

Name: _____   Symbol: _____

Name: _____   Symbol: _____

Name: _____   Symbol: _____

Name: _____   Symbol: _____

Name: _____   Symbol: _____

Name: _____   Symbol: _____

Part 2. Track your stock's performance using the chart below. Record daily activity associated with your specific stock, including the number of shares traded, as well as any profits or losses.

Stock: _____

Date	Price Per Share	Shares Held	High	Low	Change	Shares Sold	Profit or Loss

Wall Street (continued)

Part 3. Using the information from your chart in Part 2, create a line graph to illustrate the profits and losses for your stock over the set period of time. Then, combine the information from your graph with the other team members' graphs to make one investment team graph that compares how all of your team's stocks performed over time. Create your graphs on grid paper and attach them in the space below.

Part 4. Based on how well your stock performed this week, what do you estimate your profits or losses would be over a month's time? Explain your estimations and show your work.

_____

_____

_____

_____

_____

What's Your Problem?

Directions: Select an issue or problem from your local community. Then, follow the problem-solving process outlined below to reach a solution. Make notes in the chart and use a separate sheet of paper to record your work for each step of the process.

Step 1. **Define and understand the problem.**
- What are you asked to find/solve?
- Define terms or related vocabulary.
- What type of math might be involved?

Step 2. **Gather and process information.**
- What other information do you need?
- What resources can you use to find that information?

Step 3. **Formulate a plan.**
- What is your solution?
- What steps are involved?
- What types of math will you use in your plan?

Step 4. **Implement the plan.**
- How will you carry out your plan?
- What are the possible outcomes of your plan?

Step 5. **Evaluate the plan.**
- How effective was your solution?
- Is the problem solved?

Step 6. **Share the solution.**
- How will you share your solution?

Practice Math Test—Grade 8

Name: _____

Date: _____ Class: _____

Directions: This test contains 48 math problems, a math reference chart, and an answer sheet. Read each problem carefully. Mark your answers on your answer sheet. If you do not understand a question, ask your teacher for help.

Note to Teacher: This chapter contains a reproducible practice test based on the most common math standards tested nationwide at the eighth-grade level. This practice test can be given to your students before, during, or after they have completed the activities in Chapter 5. (For a short diagnostic test, see Chapter 3.)

Practice Math Test—Grade 8 (continued)

Directions

Read each problem carefully. You will mark most answers on your answer sheet by filling in the correct bubble.

Sample 1   The school bus was $^3/_5$ empty.
What percent of the bus was empty?

A   40%

B   75%

C   25%

D   60%   **Answer:**   Ⓐ Ⓑ Ⓒ ●

For some problems, you will be asked to determine the answer and fill in a bubble grid on your answer sheet. Follow these steps:

1. Work the problem and find an answer.
2. Write your answer in the boxes across the top of the grid.
   - Print only one digit or symbol in each box.
   - Be sure to write a dollar sign, fraction bar, or decimal point in the answer box if it is part of the answer.
3. Fill in the corresponding bubble in each column.
   Do NOT fill in bubbles in the empty columns.

Sample 2   Mario bought a CD for $13.25, including tax. He paid for the CD with a $20 bill. How much change did Mario receive?

Answer: $6.75

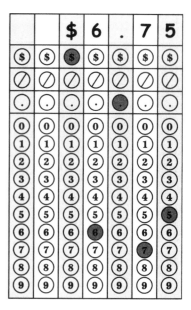

For all other types of problems, follow the directions given on the test page.

Practice Math Test—Grade 8 (continued)

Math Reference Chart — 1

Length

Customary			Metric		
1 foot	=	12 inches	1 centimeter	=	10 millimeters
1 yard	=	3 feet	1 meter	=	100 centimeters
1 mile	=	1,760 yards	1 kilometer	=	1,000 meters
1 mile	=	5,280 feet			

Mass and Weight

Customary			Metric		
1 pound	=	16 ounces	1 gram	=	1,000 milligrams
1 ton	=	2,000 pounds	1 kilogram	=	1,000 grams

Capacity and Volume

Customary			Metric		
1 cup	=	8 ounces	1 milliliter	=	1 cubic centimeter
1 pint	=	2 cups	1 liter	=	1,000 milliliters
1 quart	=	2 pints			
1 gallon	=	4 quarts			

Time

1 minute	=	60 seconds	1 year	=	365 days
1 hour	=	60 minutes	1 year	=	52 weeks
1 day	=	24 hours	1 year	=	12 months
1 week	=	7 days			

Simple Interest

$$I = prt$$

I	=	interest
p	=	principal
r	=	rate
t	=	time

continued on next page

Practice Math Test—Grade 8 (continued)

Math Reference Chart — 2

Key

l = length	P = perimeter	A = area
w = width	SA = surface area	V = volume
s = length of a side	d = diameter	B = area of the base of a solid
b = base	r = radius	
h = height	C = circumference	$\pi \approx 3.14$ or $\frac{22}{7}$

The sum of the interior angles of a polygon is equal to $180(n - 2)$, where n is the number of sides in the polygon.

Perimeter

square $P = 4s$

rectangle $P = 2(l + w)$

Circumference

circle $C = 2\pi r$ or πd

Pythagorean Theorem

$a^2 + b^2 = c^2$

Area

□	square	$A = s^2$
▭	rectangle	$A = lw$ or bh
△	triangle	$A = \frac{1}{2}bh$ or $\frac{bh}{2}$
▱	trapezoid	$A = \frac{1}{2}(b_1 + b_2)h$ or $\frac{(b_1 + b_2)h}{2}$
▱	parallelogram	$A = bh$
○	circle	$A = \pi r^2$

Surface Area

	cube	$SA = 6s^2$
	rectangular solid	$SA = 2(lw) + 2(hw) + 2(lh)$
	cylinder (total)	$SA = 2\pi rh + 2\pi r^2$
	sphere	$SA = 4\pi r^2$

Volume

	rectangular solid	$V = lwh$
	prism	$V = Bh$
	cylinder	$V = \pi r^2 h$
	pyramid	$V = \frac{1}{3}Bh$
	sphere	$V = \frac{4}{3}\pi r^3$

Practice Math Test—Grade 8

1 Which rational number is the multiplicative inverse of $5\frac{1}{3}$?

   A $^{16}/_3$

   B $^3/_{16}$

   C $^{-16}/_3$

   D $^{-3}/_{16}$

2 Sarah recorded 5 temperatures during a winter week in her city. Which list shows the temperatures in order from coolest to warmest?

   F   -2° F, -16° F, 0° F, 28° F, 32° F

   G   32° F, 28° F, 0° F, -16° F, -2° F

   H   -16° F, -2° F, 0° F, 28° F, 32° F

   J   -2° F, 0° F, -16° F, 28° F, 32° F

3 Which value of x will make the equation below true?

$$4^x = 256$$

   A   6

   B   5

   C   4

   D   3

4 A new, high-tech cell phone costs $399. It costs $90 more than twice the cost of an older model. The cost of the older cell phone model (m) can be represented by the equation $2m + 90 = 399$. What is the price of the older cell phone model?

Record your answer in the bubble grid below and on your answer sheet. Write your answer across the top and fill in the corresponding bubbles in each column.

5 A box is shaped like a cube with an edge that is 3 feet long. What is the volume of the box?

   F   9 ft.^{3}

   G   18 ft.^{3}

   H   27 ft.^{3}

   J   36 ft.^{3}

GO ON

6 The drawing shows a solid figure built with cubes.

Which drawing below represents the solid figure as viewed from directly above?

A

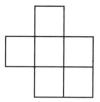

B

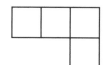

C

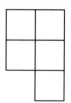

D

7 The graph below shows the number of eighth-grade students who have played for the soccer club teams at Alamo Middle School for the past 5 years.

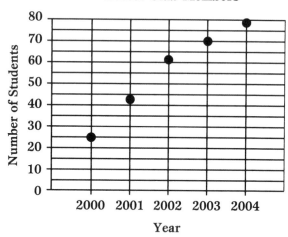

Which is the best estimate of the total number of eighth-grade students participating in the soccer club from 2000 through 2004?

F 140

G 190

H 250

J 280

GO ON

8 The chart shows how many football mums a flower shop sold in 4 months.

Flower Shop Sales for Football Mums

Month	Number of Mums Sold
September	235
October	372
November	568
December	175

Which is the best estimate of the total number of football mums sold in October and November combined?

A 600

B 750

C 950

D 1,200

9 Shane is taking a cooking class and must arrange measurements of flour in order from smallest to largest. Which list of flour measurements is in the correct order?

F $\frac{1}{4}$ c., $\frac{2}{3}$ c., $\frac{1}{2}$ c., $\frac{5}{8}$ c.

G $\frac{5}{8}$ c., $\frac{1}{4}$ c., $\frac{2}{3}$ c., $\frac{1}{2}$ c.

H $\frac{1}{2}$ c., $\frac{1}{4}$ c., $\frac{2}{3}$ c., $\frac{5}{8}$ c.

J $\frac{1}{4}$ c., $\frac{1}{2}$ c., $\frac{5}{8}$ c., $\frac{2}{3}$ c.

10 The graph below shows that the rectangle Q'R'S'T' is a dilation of rectangle QRST.

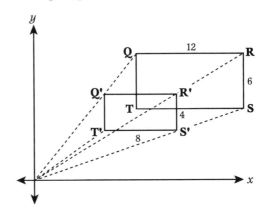

What is the scale factor used to create rectangle Q'R'S'T'?

A $\frac{1}{2}$

B $\frac{1}{3}$

C $\frac{2}{3}$

D $\frac{3}{4}$

11 A Pikeral frog lays up to 3,000 eggs at the edge of a pond in shallow water. If about 3% of the eggs survive to become tadpoles, how many eggs will grow to become tadpoles?

F 9

G 90

H 300

J 900

GO ON

Practice Math Test—Grade 8 (continued)

12 The Riverwood school district wants to build a new middle school to accommodate school overcrowding. After doing a study, the district found that the two suburbs with the highest growth in new home construction were Westview and Arlington Heights. The table on the right shows their growth from 1985 through 2000.

Which line graph below best represents the data in the table?

New Construction Data
(Number of Homes Built)

Year	Westview	Arlington Heights
1985	286	342
1990	421	563
1995	968	897
2000	1,267	1,325

A **New Construction**

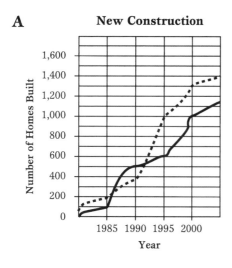

B **New Construction**

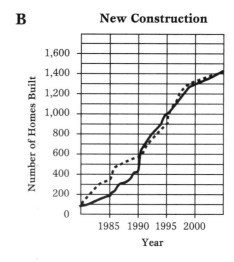

- - = Westview
— = Arlington Hights

C **New Construction**

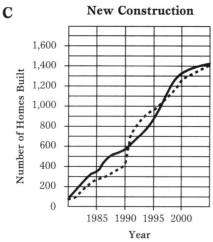

D **New Construction**

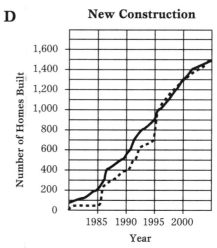

GO ON

13 Which is equivalent to $(3 \times 5^2)^3$?

F 3×5^5

G $3^3 \times 5^6$

H $3^2 \times 5^5$

J $3^3 \times 5^5$

14 Mike built a fence around his dog Rex's doghouse to keep Rex from running away. The dimensions of the fenced-in area are shown in the diagram below.

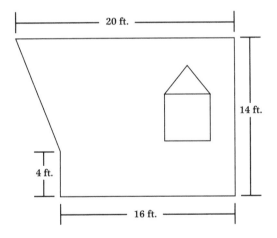

What is the total area, in square feet, enclosed by the fence?

A 244 ft.^{2}

B 252 ft.^{2}

C 264 ft.^{2}

D 280 ft.^{2}

15 Principal Jackson has a box containing the names of students who remained on the honor roll for every class all year. The box contains the names of 25 eighth graders, 15 seventh graders, and 10 sixth graders. Mr. Jackson is going to randomly draw the name of a student from the box to receive a prize. What is the probability that a seventh grader will receive the prize?

F 50%

G 30%

H 20%

J 15%

16 Mr. Ashford took out a $7,000 car loan at an annual simple interest rate of 6.7%. If he paid off the loan in 24 months, which expression can be used to find the total amount of interest he paid on the loan?

A 7,000 – 0.067 × 2

B 7,000 × 0.067 ÷ 24

C 7,000 × 0.067 + 24

D 7,000 × 0.067 × 2

GO ON ⟹

Practice Math Test—Grade 8 (continued)

17   Which number line shows the solution to the inequality $-9 < y < 2$?

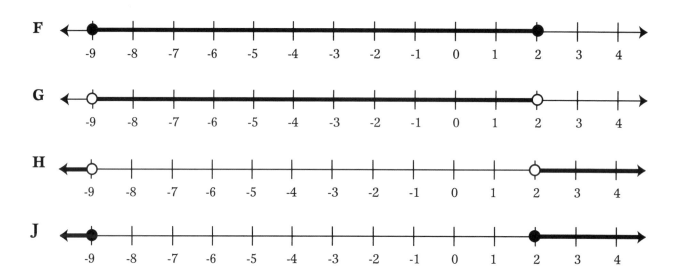

18   Olivia's family plans to drive 130 miles from their hometown of Seaport to Stockton, and then 145 miles further to Smithville. Olivia calculated the straight-line distance from Smithville to her hometown to be about 275 miles.

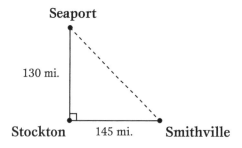

Which formula can be used to determine if Olivia's answer is correct?

A   area of a triangle

B   Pythagorean theorem

C   perimeter of a triangle

D   diameter of a rectangle

19 Simon wants to measure the height of a window as shown in the drawing below.

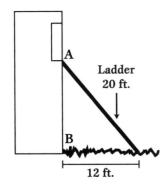

If a ladder leaning against the building is 20 feet long, what is the distance from point A, the bottom of the window, to point B, the ground?

F   12 ft.

G   16 ft.

H   18 ft.

J   20 ft.

20 The girls' volleyball team at Springdale Middle School has played nine games so far this season. In those nine games, they scored 25, 15, 13, 25, 15, 9, 11, 14, and 15 points.

Which statement below is accurate?

A   mean = mode

B   mean < mode

C   median = mode

D   median < mode

21 Which property does the equation below demonstrate?

$$8(4 + 7) = 32 + 56$$

F   commutative

G   identity

H   associative

J   distributive

22 Large apples are on sale for $1.88 per pound. Each apple weighs about $1/3$ pound. Which is the best estimate for the cost of 50 apples?

A $10

B $20

C $30

D $40

23 A drawing of a new amusement park uses a scale of 1 cm = 200 m. The tracks for the train that takes visitors around the park is drawn as 47 cm long. How many meters is the actual length of the train tracks?

F   2,470 m

G   4,700 m

H   9,000 m

J   9,400 m

GO ON

Practice Math Test—Grade 8 (continued)

24 The width of the rectangle below is represented by a certain positive number p. Its length is represented by $p + 4$.

p

$p + 4$

Which expression represents the area of the rectangle?

A $p(p + 4)$

B $p + (p + 4)$

C $2p + 2(p + 4)$

D $2p + (p + 4)$

25 The Spanish club is planning to make nachos to sell at the school's spring festival. They will need 2 bags of corn chips to make a dozen orders of nachos. Each bag of corn chips costs $2.75. The Spanish club wants to make and sell 10 dozen orders of nachos. Which expression shows how much it will cost the Spanish club to buy enough corn chips to make the nachos?

F $12 \times 10 \times \$2.75$

G $(10 - 2) \times \$2.75$

H $2 \times 10 \times \$2.75$

J $(12 \div 2) \times \$2.75$

26 Light travels at a speed of about 18,000,000,000 meters per minute. Express this number in scientific notation.

A 1.8×10^9

B $.18 \times 10^{10}$

C 18×10^9

D 1.8×10^{10}

27 The eighth graders at Dale Middle School voted on a new school mascot. Based on the graph, which 2 mascots combined received fewer votes than the winning mascot?

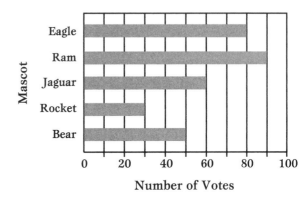

New School Mascot

F jaguar and rocket

G ram and eagle

H rocket and bear

J bear and jaguar

GO ON

28 Jake wants to buy 3 items that total $170 before tax. If sales tax is 8%, how much will he pay for the items, including tax?

Record your answer in the bubble grid below and on your answer sheet. Write your answer across the top and fill in the corresponding bubbles in each column.

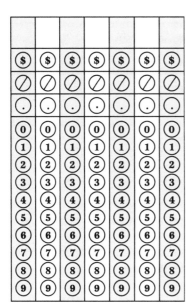

29 What is the missing number in this sequence?

3, 7, 13, 21, ___, 43, 57, 73

A   27

B   31

C   32

D   40

30 The two figures below are congruent. All angles in the two figures are right angles.

Figure 1

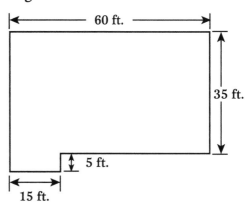

Figure 2

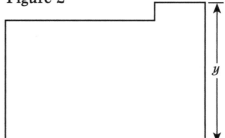

What is the length of side y in Figure 2?

F   45 ft.

G   40 ft.

H   35 ft.

J   15 ft.

GO ON

31 Mrs. Rigby wants to buy a sailboat. The savings and loan company will lend her $6,000 at a 5.8% interest rate. Mrs. Rigby must make monthly payments to pay back the amount she borrows. What information is needed to calculate her monthly payment?

A The amount of money Mrs. Rigby has for a down payment

B The total number of payments Mrs. Rigby will make

C Mrs. Rigby's monthly salary

D The size and model of boat Mrs. Rigby will buy

32 Keisha wants to cut a piece of wrapping paper to wrap the box-shaped gift below. What is the surface area of the box?

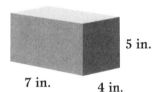

5 in.

7 in.   4 in.

F 16 in.²

G 126 in.²

H 140 in.²

J 166 in.²

33 The chart below shows the scores of each gymnast in 3 rounds of one tournament event. The scoring scale is 1 to 6, with 6 being the highest score possible.

Tournament Scores

Gymnast	Round 1	Round 2	Round 3
Kelly	5.4	4.8	5.6
Lana	5.1	5.5	5.8
Tina	5.7	5.2	5.5
Sandra	5.3	5.5	5.6
Danielle	5.7	5.7	5.4
Breen	5.7	5.5	5.8
Chris	5.5	5.1	4.9

Which of the following statements is NOT supported by the data shown in the chart?

A Chris had the lowest mean score.

B Breen had the best mean score.

C Danielle's mean score equals the mode score.

D Lana's and Sandra's mean scores were tied.

GO ON

Practice Math Test—Grade 8 (continued)

34 If n represents the position of a number in this sequence, which expression identifies the pattern?

Position	1st	2nd	3rd	4th	...	nth
Value of the Term	1	7	25	79	...	

F $3^n + 2$

G $3^n - 2$

H $4^n - n$

J $2^n + 1$

---

35 Carl wants to tile his kitchen floor with a pattern of similar rectangular tiles. Each tile Carl has is 3 inches wide and 5 inches long. He wants to cut down some of the tiles to be only 1.5 inches wide. Using the same scale, how long should the smaller tiles be?

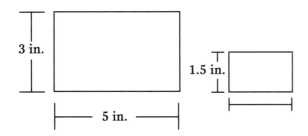

3 in.

5 in.

1.5 in.

A   1.5 in.

B   2.5 in.

C   3.5 in.

D   4.5 in.

36 EZ Pack shipping company sells two types of cartons that are shaped like rectangular prisms.

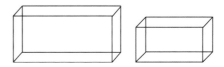

The larger carton has a volume of 960 cubic inches. The smaller carton has dimensions that are half the size of the larger carton. What is the volume, in cubic inches, of the smaller carton?

F   120 in.^{3}

G   240 in.^{3}

H   360 in.^{3}

J   480 in.^{3}

GO ON

Practice Math Test—Grade 8 (continued)

37 The school orchestra has a total of 57 members. The table shows the number of instruments of each type in the orchestra.

Musical Instruments in the School Orchestra

Type of Instrument	Number of Instruments
Violin	20
Viola	14
Cello	10
Bass	3
Flute	6
Clarinet	4

Which graph best represents the data in the table?

A

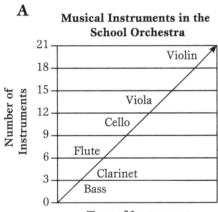

Musical Instruments in the School Orchestra

B

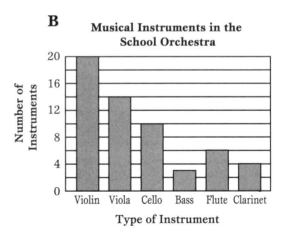

Musical Instruments in the School Orchestra

C

Musical Instruments in the School Orchestra

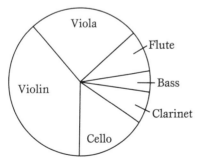

D

Musical Instruments in the School Orchestra

Practice Math Test—Grade 8 (continued)

38 Ms. D'Angelo's math students measured and recorded their heights on a chart in the classroom. Sandy's height was 1.54 meters. What is another way to show Sandy's height?

F 0.154 cm

G 15.4 cm

H 154 cm

J 1,540 cm

39 The graph below shows how Carolyn spent her time last week reshelving fiction books as a library aide. If she reshelved 30 science fiction books, how many suspense books did she reshelve?

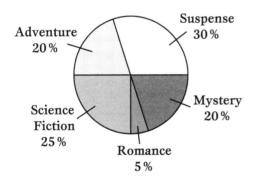

A 120

B 35

C 40

D 36

40 In the spinner below, the pointer stopped on the shaded region.

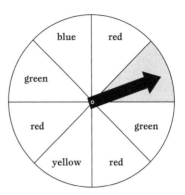

What color should the shaded region be so that the probability of the pointer landing on this color is $1/2$?

F red

G blue

H yellow

J green

41 The aquatic center's swimming pool is shaped like a rectangular prism. The pool is 8 feet deep, 20 feet wide, and 98 feet long. If the pool is empty, how many cubic feet of water must be added to fill the pool so it is exactly half full?

A 1,960 ft.^{3}

B 5,227 ft.^{3}

C 7,840 ft.^{3}

D 15,680 ft.^{3}

Practice Math Test—Grade 8 (continued)

42 Juan earns $9.25 per hour working at an electronics store. Last week, employees earned a bonus of $50.00 for each camcorder sold. The chart shows Juan's work record for the week.

Juan's Work Record

Day Worked	Sunday	Monday	Tuesday	Wednesday	Thursday
Number of Hours	8	8	8	8	8
Number of Bonuses	2	0	1	2	1

Which equation can be used to find E, the total amount of money Juan earned for the week?

F $E = 8(9.25) + 50(6)(5)$

G $E = 9.25 + 50(8 + 6)$

H $E = 9.25(8)(5) + 50(6)$

J $E = 9.25(8)(5)(6) + 50$

---

43 Penny recorded the number of colored candies in a package. Her records show a ratio of 6 red candies for every 7 blue candies. If there were 160 blue candies in the package, which proportion could be used to find r, the number of red candies in the package?

A $^6/_7 = {}^r/_{160}$

B $^7/_6 = {}^r/_{160}$

C $^7/_{17} = {}^{160}/_r$

D $^6/_{17} = {}^r/_{160}$

44 Which point on the number line below best represents the square root of 5?

F   point W

G   point X

H   point Y

J   point Z

GO ON

     CD-2241 *Teamwork Test Prep*

45 The Junior Honor Society sold flowers for Valentine's Day as a fund-raiser. The club ordered a total of 200 roses and 350 carnations. They decided to sell each rose for $1.50 and each carnation for $0.75. The actual wholesale cost for each rose was $0.89 and each carnation was $0.37. If the Spanish club sold a total of 198 roses and 327 carnations, what was the society's total profit, after costs, for the fund-raiser?

A $178.00

B $234.75

C $307.50

D $542.25

46 Draw the line described by the equation below on the coordinate grid. Draw the line here and on your answer sheet.

$$y = x - 5$$

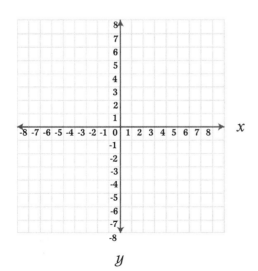

47 Nate and Julie picked peaches at a local orchard. Nate picked $1/3$ of the peaches that were on one tree. Julie picked $1/2$ of the peaches that were left on the tree. After Julie finished, there were 165 peaches left on the tree. How many peaches were on the tree when Nate and Julie began?

F   990

G   495

H   330

J   165

48 To make 3 dozen cupcakes, a recipe calls for 2 eggs and $1\frac{1}{2}$ cups of sugar. Paula wants to make 12 dozen cupcakes for the student council bake sale. How many eggs and how many cups of sugar does Paula need?

A   4 eggs, 3 cups of sugar

B   8 eggs, 6 cups of sugar

C   12 eggs, 8 cups of sugar

D   24 eggs, 18 cups of sugar

STOP

END OF PRACTICE TEST

Practice Math Test—Grade 8
Answer Sheet

Directions: Mark your answers on this answer sheet. Be sure to fill in each bubble completely and erase any stray marks.

1 Ⓐ Ⓑ Ⓒ Ⓓ

2 Ⓕ Ⓖ Ⓗ Ⓙ

3 Ⓐ Ⓑ Ⓒ Ⓓ

4 Write your answer across the top of the bubble grid. Fill in the corresponding bubbles in each column.

Ⓢ	Ⓢ	Ⓢ	Ⓢ	Ⓢ	Ⓢ	Ⓢ
⊘	⊘	⊘	⊘	⊘	⊘	⊘
⊙	⊙	⊙	⊙	⊙	⊙	⊙
⓪	⓪	⓪	⓪	⓪	⓪	⓪
①	①	①	①	①	①	①
②	②	②	②	②	②	②
③	③	③	③	③	③	③
④	④	④	④	④	④	④
⑤	⑤	⑤	⑤	⑤	⑤	⑤
⑥	⑥	⑥	⑥	⑥	⑥	⑥
⑦	⑦	⑦	⑦	⑦	⑦	⑦
⑧	⑧	⑧	⑧	⑧	⑧	⑧
⑨	⑨	⑨	⑨	⑨	⑨	⑨

5 Ⓕ Ⓖ Ⓗ Ⓙ

6 Ⓐ Ⓑ Ⓒ Ⓓ

7 Ⓕ Ⓖ Ⓗ Ⓙ

8 Ⓐ Ⓑ Ⓒ Ⓓ

9 Ⓕ Ⓖ Ⓗ Ⓙ

10 Ⓐ Ⓑ Ⓒ Ⓓ

11 Ⓕ Ⓖ Ⓗ Ⓙ

12 Ⓐ Ⓑ Ⓒ Ⓓ

13 Ⓕ Ⓖ Ⓗ Ⓙ

14 Ⓐ Ⓑ Ⓒ Ⓓ

15 Ⓕ Ⓖ Ⓗ Ⓙ

16 Ⓐ Ⓑ Ⓒ Ⓓ

17 Ⓕ Ⓖ Ⓗ Ⓙ

18 Ⓐ Ⓑ Ⓒ Ⓓ

19 Ⓕ Ⓖ Ⓗ Ⓙ

20 Ⓐ Ⓑ Ⓒ Ⓓ

21 Ⓕ Ⓖ Ⓗ Ⓙ

22 Ⓐ Ⓑ Ⓒ Ⓓ

23 Ⓕ Ⓖ Ⓗ Ⓙ

24 Ⓐ Ⓑ Ⓒ Ⓓ

25 Ⓕ Ⓖ Ⓗ Ⓙ

26 Ⓐ Ⓑ Ⓒ Ⓓ

27 Ⓕ Ⓖ Ⓗ Ⓙ

Practice Math Test—Grade 8 (continued)

Answer Sheet

28 Write your answer across the top of the bubble grid. Fill in the corresponding bubbles in each column.

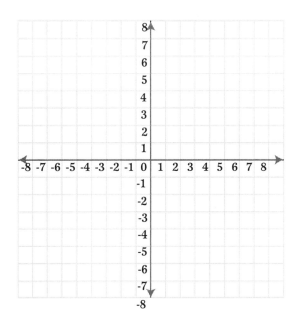

29 Ⓐ Ⓑ Ⓒ Ⓓ

30 Ⓕ Ⓖ Ⓗ Ⓙ

31 Ⓐ Ⓑ Ⓒ Ⓓ

32 Ⓕ Ⓖ Ⓗ Ⓙ

33 Ⓐ Ⓑ Ⓒ Ⓓ

34 Ⓕ Ⓖ Ⓗ Ⓙ

35 Ⓐ Ⓑ Ⓒ Ⓓ

36 Ⓕ Ⓖ Ⓗ Ⓙ

37 Ⓐ Ⓑ Ⓒ Ⓓ

38 Ⓕ Ⓖ Ⓗ Ⓙ

39 Ⓐ Ⓑ Ⓒ Ⓓ

40 Ⓕ Ⓖ Ⓗ Ⓙ

41 Ⓐ Ⓑ Ⓒ Ⓓ

42 Ⓕ Ⓖ Ⓗ Ⓙ

43 Ⓐ Ⓑ Ⓒ Ⓓ

44 Ⓕ Ⓖ Ⓗ Ⓙ

45 Ⓐ Ⓑ Ⓒ Ⓓ

46 Draw the line described by the equation on the coordinate grid.

$$y = x - 5$$

47 Ⓕ Ⓖ Ⓗ Ⓙ

48 Ⓐ Ⓑ Ⓒ Ⓓ

page 19
Diagnostic Math Test

1 A		**2** H	
3 C		**4** F	
5 A		**6** H	
7 B		**8** H	
9 C			

10

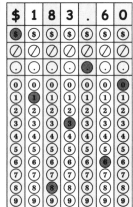

11 H		**12** C	
13 F		**14** A	
15 F		**16** C	

17

18 J

page 91
Practice Math Test

1 B	**2** H	**3** C	

4
$ 1 5 4 . 5 0

5 H	**6** B	**7** J	
8 C	**9** J	**10** C	
11 G	**12** C	**13** G	
14 A	**15** G	**16** D	
17 G	**18** B	**19** G	
20 C	**21** J	**22** C	
23 J	**24** A	**25** H	
26 D	**27** H		

28
$ 1 8 3 . 6 0

29 B	**30** G	**31** B
32 J	**33** C	**34** G
35 B	**36** F	**37** B
38 H	**39** D	**40** F
41 C	**42** H	**43** A
44 G	**45** B	

46

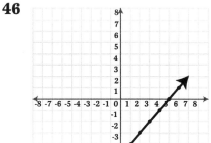

47 G	**48** B